Max
My Father

*Portrait of Max painted by Per Hurum in Helsingfors
(Helsinki) in 1930–1 (in the family's possession). Photo
by Anna Christmas.*

MAX
My Father

The story of Captain
Maximilian Carden Despard,
DSC, RN (1892–1964)

ANNABELLE DESPARD

PORTAL

© Portal Books 2014

ISBN 978-82-8314-026-2

Design and cover: Lars Aase
Paper: Serixo 120 gr/m^2
Printed by InPrint, Latvia
Photos: Sigve Mathisen

Any inquiry on this book should be addressed to:
Portal Books
Gimlemoen 19
4630 Kristiansand
Norway
www.portalforlag.no
post@portalforlag.no

Contents

Acknowledgements

I wish to thank Olav Asgard, Keith and Marianne Brown, Henry Despard, John Despard, Minda Despard, Richard Despard, Sonya Despard, Jeffrey Evans, Emma Fischel, Jonathan Green, Kristian Hagestad, Annette Hurum, Gillian Jones, Simon and Sarah King, Jelena Loma, Ian Maitland, Sigve Mathisen, Marianne Mays, Jonathan Moffatt, Pål Repstad, Richard Scott and Jardar Seim for their kind help.

Without the help of Patrick Newman and Patrick Despard this book would never have been published. My sister Anita has followed the progress of this book since it started, but it is above all my brother Herbert I have to thank for his invaluable sources, information, comments, anecdotes and encouragement.

The Black Box

There are many ways of not having a father. Some fathers are dead, some in prison, some divorced. Some were never present at all. Other people I knew had fathers; friendly or formidable, they were present. My father was certainly not dead; not for a long time. Nor was he present; not for long. He was not dead, but not part of my life. I was not quite an orphan; the situation was unclear.

Who was he? My quest started when my eldest brother Terence died in 2008. Terence was an old man by then so it was a sad but not tragic death. I wished to say something in the church and I thought it would be a good point of departure to start with Terence's middle name, Broke (pronounced 'Brook'). I knew this name was connected with something heroic and splendid, but did not really know what. So I had to find out. I discovered the *Broke* was one of two destroyers involved in 1917 in one of the more successful actions of the First World War. My father was First Lieutenant and the captain was Teddy Evans, already famous from Scott's Antarctic expeditions, but from then on called 'Evans of the *Broke*.'

We have a letter written in pencil in large sprawling writing. It is from Max, my father, in hospital after he was badly wounded in a gunnery accident in 1925, asking his father to tell young Terence that they were patching him together like a jigsaw puzzle. My task in writing the story of my father is similar, for I am trying to piece together the story of a man I knew so little. In his last years he told me that 'they' kept asking him to write his memoirs. I was too young to ask who 'they' were and what he would write about. Nor did I encourage him to tell me. This book is an attempt to make up for that omission. It is an attempt to pick my way through the decades, through an assortment of information, looking for a father. I had never been told much about him; nor had I asked, as there were often odd looks and silences when I approached my grandmother or my brothers and sister. I had the impression that he was a hero, but that something had gone wrong.

As I knew so little, I had to approach the task as if it were a school assignment, relying on sources. There were more than I expected; several books and memoirs mentioned my father and there were also the biographies of better-known family members. And we had family papers. I have made serious efforts to obtain permission to quote from published sources. I have tried to get the facts right, but I cannot pretend that it is an academic book; it relies too much on anecdote. I am no historian and I feel I have been skirting the edges of historical enquiry; there are doubtless many more sources that could have been explored. I hope one day someone will continue the search.

'We'll get the black box,' my brother Herbert said. Herbert is older than me and my chief informant. He provides facts and Apocrypha, as family anecdotes tend to live a life of their own and solidify into something fact-like. Herbert is the custodian of the family papers and has in his safe keeping a large black box labelled 'MAX.' This was now ceremoniously brought out. It is full of photographs of boys in uniform, men in uniform, men on deck and on shore. All unnamed. And there is Max, unmistakable, in a variety of uniforms according to his rank and the climate. To judge from these photographs, we would suppose he spent his whole life in uniform or brandishing variously tennis-racquets, golf clubs, skis. One picture shows him with skis – on a boat. He is photographed in tweeds and in a bathing suit. He is beautiful.

The box also contains papers. In the elegant drawing-room in Herbert and Minda's London house a card-table was set up. It was a spindly work table and Herbert is a large man, but he and I worked together there, companionably sifting through testimonials, applications, reports and letters. I have seen TV programmes where people painstakingly seek out their ancestors, looking in church registers for the mention of a name. We had a wealth of documentation. Ours was not a literary family, but it was literate. We have a pile of letters Max wrote to his father H.J. Despard, Chief Constable of Lanarkshire. Max's letters were a revelation: although his spelling was somewhat irregular, he wrote concise prose, with his opinions shining through in forthright language. Almost every week he wrote to his father, mainly about his work and finances. My grandfather kept the letters: my father may have kept the replies, but they have disappeared. Yet there are huge gaps in Max's correspondence and we do not have the letters his father sent to him. There is nothing about the death of my father's younger brother Geoffrey. I didn't even know Geoffrey had existed until I started this investigation. There is no letter about the death of my grandparents, no funeral service records. My mother wrote diligently to her mother, but I have no letter from my parents to each other. There are gaps and silences. I have no letters from the time of my mother's death.

I have a small chocolate-box of letters myself from my father's last years. They are never marked by the year, but it is possible to date them by the many changes of address.

I was born in 1943. My father was born in 1892, so he was well over fifty when I appeared as an afterthought. My two brothers

Terence and Herbert and my sister Anita were all born in the 1920s and were respectively twenty-one, fifteen and sixteen years older than me. They had memories of my father that I could not share, while all I remember is a mild old man with a walking-stick. He wore friendly smelling tweeds. Most people remember seeing their father in various outfits; I cannot remember ever seeing him in his bathing suit or in uniform.

The years 1949 and 1950 were unhappy ones for the family. Fortunately for me they are more or less wiped from my memory. I only know I behaved badly at times, and, being a generally peaceful person, I assume I was unhappy. Max and I parted company in February 1951. As I was only seven years old this was not a mutual separation. I don't think he wanted it either. Events forced it and decisions were made somewhere. I went to stay with my mother's family in Norway and when I came back to England in 1953 I did not live with him or see him very often. So the memories I have are few. I remember him quarrelling with Terence at every meal. This was upsetting, but I never blamed my father for anything.

'I didn't know my father,' Anita said. 'People didn't then.' Anita has a large family of her own and has never been very interested in ancient family history. She also has unhappy memories. I am lucky; I remember my father's tenderness. Perhaps unusually for a father in those days, especially one from the Victorian age, he helped me so that I did not fall into the vast mahogany-surrounded lavatory in the upstairs bathroom. He also let me sit in his study, where I could sit quietly with my favourite book of Scottish tartans. He sat in his armchair with antimacassar or he sat at his desk.

He called me 'Sweetie-pie.'

I have no idea what he did at his desk. Perhaps he was thinking about starting the memoirs: most probably he was writing letters and paying bills. As far as I could see he never really did any work, though we lived on a farm, near Southampton. We were not real farmers, and the house was much too big for the farm. My earliest memories are of this farm and the house and I can think of no lovelier place on earth. It was called Bartley Manor.

'You must read Jane Despard's memoirs,' Herbert said. 'She wrote them in 1838.' I was not interested. I had just found a bleak death certificate – my mother's. 'Time for lunch,' Herbert said, and so we went down.

'There was something so romantic about your father,' Minda said as she made lunch. 'Romantic' did not mean that he was melancholy or poetic in any way; far from it. He was the opposite of an aesthete: he was practical and down-to-earth. However, there was so much adventure associated with him, a certain mystery, his impressive height and good looks. 'He was a great big admiral of a man,' Herbert's friend Giles Pollock said.

I will set down some facts about my father. There is no such thing as a 'bare' fact; all facts have trails of other facts and a nimbus of emotion. These are therefore brief statements:

Maximilian Carden Despard was born in 1892.
He trained at the Royal Naval College, Dartmouth from 1905.
He was First Lieutenant to Captain Teddy Evans and took part in the engagement of the Broke in April 1917.
He served in the Balkans in the 1920s, seconded to the Foreign Office.
He was seriously wounded in a gunnery accident in 1925.
He retired from the Royal Navy in 1928 and retrained as a diplomat.
He was Defence Attaché in Finland from 1929 to 1934.
He was Naval Attaché in Belgrade and Bucharest from 1938 to

1941, with 'wide duties' (the James Bond bit).

He was arrested in Kotor in 1941 and interned in Italy.

From 1942 he was Chief of Staff, Royal Navy Western Approaches Command, Cardiff.

After the war he and Terence bought the farm Bartley Manor.

He died in November 1964.

There is another parallel set of facts:

He was a sailor.

My mother was seasick.

He had four children.

He was twice widowed and three times married.

His last years were sad.

A man's life is best summed up in review. Facts, events such as the above, were affectionately conveyed in the obituary that follows, written by P.M. Maitland, former Member of Parliament for Lanark, later Earl of Lauderdale, Lord Maitland. When he first met my father he was Patrick Maitland, *The Times*'s correspondent in the Balkans. In his book *European Dateline* (1946) he gives a firsthand account of the dramatic events of 1941. The obituary was sent to Aunt Margery, Max's half-sister, but arrived too late to get into *The Times*. Again my father somehow missed out. His death went largely unnoticed.

[Copy of letter of appreciation written by the Master of Lauderdale: the Honourable P. Maitland, MP]
Captain Maximilian Carden Despard D.S.C., R.N. who died recently will long live in the memory of his War time friends as the redoubt-able "Skipper Despard" Naval Attaché in Belgrade and Bucharest

during the last War and a figure of commanding humour, kindness and courage. At the end of his life it was daily necessary to dress an open wound sustained in the explosion in H.M.S. Harebell in 1925. His service and Post War Career were together of such drama but also secrecy that few of his friends knew the whole story of his adventures and he was personally reluctant to talk about them. He was First Lieutenant to Evans of the Broke in the First World War and was at the side of Evans in the boarding operation known to naval historians. His active naval service continued until he fell victim to the Harebell gunnery accident but shortly afterwards he joined the Danube Commission and became a well known figure all the way from the upper reaches above Budapest down to Constanza. One of the specialised interests as a Danube Commission member was the Iron Gates Narrows between Roumania and Jugoslavia. His expert knowledge of this and other features of Danube hydrography stood him in good stead, on the outbreak of the Second World War, he was named Naval Attaché to Bucharest and Belgrade together. This writer remembers him best for those few years of war time in neutral countries where his striding figure and social gaiety vividly belied the common talk of enemy propaganda that Britain was defeated before she began and the British people were now down at heel and effete. He showed conspicuous courage during the bombing of Belgrade in March 1941, but after an ineffectual attempt to get through to Greece and the Middle East as the German Armies closed in he was captured along with the staff of the British legation in Jugoslavia down on the Dalmatian Coast and interned by the Italian Government. During this time he cheered and led his party with a courage and sagacity that horrified the professional diplomats in the party; but brought solace and hope to a motley crowd of some hundred British subjects whose eventual release from internment and despatch in a sealed train across Vichy and occupied France to Madrid, was a minor Odyssey.

In 1920 he married Leonora, daughter of J. Wardrop Moore Esq., of Greenhall, Lanarkshire, by whom he had one son.

She died of an illness contracted after a skiing accident at Adelboden, Switzerland. Ever after he made a regular gift of skis to the village school in Adelboden in her memory. Later he married Lilanna, Daughter of J. Hurum Esq., of Oslo, Norway, by whom he had one son and two daughters. She died in 1949.

He married in 1952 Mrs Nixon by whom he is survived.

The inactivity of the post war years were to him as pain and labour, he found it increasingly hard in later years to get used to the life of an ex. Naval officer dwelling in a country backwater. But those who knew him to the end will long remember the laughter that came with his every reminiscence, they reached back to his boyhood days in Lanarkshire where he is still remembered as the desperado son of a distinguished Chief Constable.

Minda and Herbert visiting the ruins of Despard houses in Ireland in the 1960s.

Family

The first years I recall were in the New Forest. The New Forest was lovely; Bartley village was not. The houses, mainly bungalows, were built along the road. 'Ribbon development' I think it is called, but it was more like a piece of string. However, the place had great attractions for me: there was a village hall with a tin roof, where I was not allowed to learn tap-dancing; and a chapel where I was not allowed to go to Sunday school. My parents had pre-war habits (which war?) and I was not allowed to play with children from the village. Not surprisingly I thought we were very grand. I assumed we had lived in the house for centuries, but we had only lived there for two years. The shooting-sticks, guns and fishing-rods imparted a sense of permanence. However, the impedimenta of the upper classes are movable, ready to stake out territory in new places whenever called for.

'You must write about the Hugheses,' Herbert said. Why should I? I did not know who they were, and I was just getting on the trail of my father through clues in the black box. I was concerned with recent generations. The past is so crowded. It unnerves me; all those unknown people, jostling soundlessly to get a mite of attention. Then from a drawer Herbert brought out the family tree. It was huge, resembling some kind of map of the Underground (which I suppose it was), only the stations all had names like John, William, George and James, while the junctions and branch lines included many Gertrudes.

What can our ancestors tell us? The answer is easy: they tell us what we want to hear. If their features please us, we claim kinship. If we disapprove, we ignore them. They do not impose themselves on us and they expect nothing of us. Or do they? We should perhaps give them their due by at least trying to find out who they were.

How important were the Despards? These things are measured on a sliding scale, and I don't think we were very impressive. No one in the family was titled, though Aunt Margery was related by marriage to the Hamiltons of Emma Hamilton and Lord Nelson fame, but I cannot remember a fuss being made of this. However, we did have a crest, worn on signet-rings, and our Huguenot ancestor was inscribed in the Roll of the Huguenots. To understand why we have a French-sounding name and why there is such a strong link to Ireland we need to go quite far back. Before the Despards became Despards they were d'Espards in France, a military family, *epard* being an archaic word for sword. They became Huguenots, Protestants in a strongly Catholic country. We have always been proud of the Roll of the Huguenots and that our first ancestor to come from France, Philip (or Philippe?) d'Espard, was inscribed and recorded in Canterbury Cathedral. However, one click on the internet tells us that this impressive scroll is a nineteenth-century product, inspired by the work on Huguenots by the Scottish reformer Samuel Smiles, and 'not taken seriously by historians at all.' My first setback, one of many.

The Reformation and Counter-Reformation were terrible times. Protestantism grew rapidly in France and by 1559 perhaps as much as ten per cent of the population were French Calvinists, or Huguenots. Since the Huguenots were concentrated in the cities and among the growing middle classes, their social significance far exceeded their numbers. The worst excess of Catholic zeal was the Massacre of St Bartholomew on 24 August 1572. The attacks on Huguenots were essentially political in nature, the Pope being alarmed that his closest ally, France, might be lost to that worst of heresies, Protestantism. There was also a social side to it. The Huguenots were often envied for their wealth and there were enough Frenchmen willing to carry out the attacks on them. The slaughter was long-lasting, widespread and furious. In one week as many as 100,000 people may have perished, though estimates vary wildly. However many were actually slaughtered, in his *Historical Dictionary of Calvinism* (2011), Stuart Picken writes: 'The rivers of France were so filled with corpses that for many months no fish were eaten. In the valley of the Loire, wolves came down from the hills to feed upon the decaying bodies of the Huguenots.'

This helps us to understand the strong convictions of our family first in France, then in England and finally in Ireland. Those rivers of blood in France reinforced the Despard family's Protestantism.

Max always called himself Irish and was always described as an Irishman. This is perhaps part of his romantic aura. When I developed some kind of political awareness in the 1970s the sympathy among my friends was on the side of the Irish Republicans. They were the heroes in that terrible and surely unnecessary warfare called the Troubles. It was said that the Republicans had better songs and better movies; indeed Michael Collins made a great film hero and is considered a more exciting figure than his opposite numbers in Dublin Castle, which would include Lord French (more on whom later). As opposed to the thrifty Lowland Scot or the military Englishman, the stereotypical Irishman has a daredevil streak, a conspiratorial view of politics, a love of the grand gesture. These qualities are the stuff of romance and could well describe my father.

'Now you can read Jane Despard,' Herbert said, and produced a flat green book. I was not excited about the prospect of tracing all those Johns and Georges, but the memoirs turned out to be intriguing. I cannot vouch for their truth, but this is family tradition (Richard Despard has carried out research on early family history. See his *Cloak of Secrecy*). Jane Despard wrote them in 1838 and my grandfather had them typed up. They take us back to Philip d'Espard. He was lucky to escape from the banks of the Loire and left for England. There he was favoured by Queen Elizabeth's ministers and was recruited into Her Majesty's civil service. He was a good mathematician and was sent to Ireland as a 'commissioner for the partitioning of "forfeited" lands.' The lands were 'forfeited' or taken from Catholics and given, or rather sold, to Protestants. According to Jane this was not always as bad as it sounds: 'The Registry Office in Dublin shows more of purchase than appropriation in his acquisitions and those of his descendants, as proved in the sales and leases in perpetuity enjoyed by the more fortunate and present proprietors.' In the sixteenth century Philip d'Espard began his commission in the north of Ireland, but later settled in the south as he had been rewarded for service with property.

England was most wary of Ireland, a country which they feared bred terrorism. In the so-called 'Plantations' Protestant settlers were exported to Ireland from the Lowlands of Scotland to outnumber and suppress Roman Catholic rebels. The power in Ireland was in the hands of landowners, professionals and clergy of the established Church, i.e. the Protestant Church of Ireland. The Ascendancy is the name given to the ruling, landowning families in Ireland. Many of these were old Celtic families, but the majority were Protestants, such as the d'Espards. These felt themselves naturally superior to the poor 'bog Irish.' Jane tells us that when James II visited Ireland in 1687 'the whole family were described as Protestants and of course joined King William of glorious, pious and immortal memory, who delivered us

20

from popery, slavery, brass money and wooden shoes.' The family did well; no wooden shoes for them. In time the apostrophe was dropped and, like many of the Ascendancy, the Protestant Despards came to love Ireland more than England.

According to Jane, the family's assets included two 'very extensive properties in Queens County, Tipperary, Kildare, and Cork, &c. &c.' before her grandfather's 'most unwise disposition of them.' She estimated the annual income from those properties at £25,000, a substantial fortune in the eighteenth century, but alas, her grandfather 'leased away his property, not for gaming, drinking, or company-keeping, but to make votes for the Parnells.' (The family connection with the Parnells remains strong today.)

Family history can be dull. Leases, mortgages and deeds of sale do not capture the imagination as do illegitimate children and questionable sudden deaths, or strong religious and political convictions – of the Irish kind. Our family history is quite juicy, at least in patches. Jane was a maiden aunt who clearly wished to show that she was broad-minded, while keeping within the pale of propriety. She is forthright. She expresses pious sentiments but can also be very rude. Of her Aunt Kitty she says, 'She had long been deaf and always stupid.' Of one of her cousins she says 'he married (I cannot say how soon) a sour piece of goods like himself.' This is how she describes her maternal grandfather:

My grandfather, Croasdale, died previous to his father, and prematurely I have heard, by his leading a life common to a country gentleman of those days, more of wine than water being his beverage. […] His son's name was Pilkington, after his mother's family, familiarly called Pilky, and it is recorded that this father and son each drank a bottle of wine every day after dinner when alone, with no other conversation passing between them than 'Pilky, your health'—'Thank ye Sir.' 'Sir, your health'—'Thank ye Pilky.'

She was determined not to be prudish and took care not to omit the many Despards born on the wrong side of the blanket. She informs us that her

> uncle Green, had a son by his housekeeper, who was clerk of the parish when I was last in the Queen's Co. His father had left a sum of money to apprentice him to some trade when old enough, and the poor mother behaved very well in all other respects. After his death my aunt Despard was very good to her. I think it right when making this little memorial of those gone bye, to mention a thing of this kind, as should you hear it elsewhere, you might think I had suppressed other things also.

Despards went into the law or the Army. The most famous, or rather infamous, member of the family is Colonel Edward Marcus Despard, who was executed for treason. His brothers, however, had impeccable careers. John served with the Royal Fusiliers. He went to Quebec in 1775 where he distinguished himself. In 1779 he was appointed Adjutant-General to the Army and was at the surrender of Charleston in 1780. In 1799 he was appointed Military Governor of Nova Scotia. He had been in twenty-four engagements where two horses were shot from under him, and he was shipwrecked three times. He died in 1829. Andrew fought as a lieutenant at Concord in one of the first battles of the War of American Independence. In 1781 he was sent to the Caribbean where Edward Marcus also served.

There were also clergymen, including the nineteenth-century missionary George Pakenham Despard. He is best known through his connection with the Tierra del Fuegian Indians who had been taken to England on the first voyage of the *Beagle*. The four 'savages' were given the names York Minster, Fuega Basket, Boat Memory and Jemmy Button, the last because he had been abducted for the price of a button thrown into the canoe. When they arrived in England in 1830 they caused a sensation. After some years they were returned to their native shore with tables, chairs and full sets of cutlery. This experiment did not work very well. George Pakenham Despard's task was to find Jemmy Button, who had abandoned his tablecloths and returned to his former life. In the end George left, disillusioned. However, the first white baby born in Tierra del Fuego was christened Tomás Despard Bridges.

We have a notion that 'trade' was deemed despicable to the upper classes, but Jane approved strongly of merchants. 'There are few departments a man may show to more advantage good qualities than as a merchant, or be more useful to his fellow beings,' she wrote. This may well be a sigh of regret at the lack of financial sense in the family, as her father and many other Despards lost their fortunes in different ways. Some called Despard were altogether 'doubtful,' she wrote:

> You many judge of your uncle Henry's surprise, while at New South Wales, to see at the top of the list of convicts handed to him officially, 'Miss Anne Despard.' She was, I conjecture, a daughter of Mr. Pat Despard, a shoemaker, whose board hung out in the town of Mountrath, and who was the natural son of George Despard of Donore, an officer of Dragoons, and uncle of the present William Despard of the same place.

Henry Despard was in 1845 in charge of the British troops in the New Zealand Wars, or Maori Wars as they were once called. There was a Despard in a position of command in almost every war for over two centuries. However, Jane is more concerned with family than with strategy. In the next few lines she provides enough material for at least one Brontë novel:

> Francis Despard (Killaghy) had three sisters. The eldest married badly. Their father cared little for their education, and seemed to have no affection for them. I remember a governess there when I was with them very young and let them do whatever they pleased so as she had her bottle. The second, a very sweet, pretty girl, died of decline at nineteen. The third, a cross, little, deformed thing died unmarried, I forget when exactly.

Mountrath in the present county of Laois (sometimes spelt Leix, and pronounced 'Leash') is 'Despard country.' There are seven or eight properties that belonged to the family, some still standing, some in ruins. Herbert and Minda visited them all in the 1960s. Herbert asked where Donore was and an old man said, 'You must be a Despard.'

Andro Linklater in *An Unhusbanded Life*, his 1980 biography of suffragette Charlotte Despard, is not impressed by the family, and I quote him in full:

> The remaining Despards [after Edward Marcus] lived lives of some profligacy and little industry. Their general look on the purpose of life might have been summed up in a reply given by Marcus's brother Frank, when it was suggested he should put a certain legacy in a bank. 'No,' he said, 'it was a Godsend and I'll pitch it to the Devil.' They were extravagant, litigious and obsessive in their eccentricities. One spent a lifetime breeding miniature and quite useless

foxhounds, the size of Pekinese, and another spent his Army pay, while stationed at Gibraltar, buying rotten eggs to throw at the Jews. Most confined their enthusiasm to hunting and claret, and their lives within the limits of the family estates at Mountrath in the centre of Ireland. They married Wellesleys, Pakenhams and each other with monotonous regularity, and three successive generations of George Despard married three successive Gertrude Cardens, the last of whom produced Maximilian Carden. [Not my father, but my grandfather's uncle.] The Cardens introduced a strain of chronic ill-health which afflicted that branch of the family, and the marriage of Maximilian's parents was considered extremely unwise since the Carden and Despard lines were by then so interwoven as to raise anxieties about inbreeding.

Linklater's racy account is very much at odds with the impression I have of a Protestant family who took up the civic duties of the ruling class. His version would be more convincing if it were accurate. For instance, very small 'foxhounds' are most likely beagles. He also takes stories out of context. Jane does not deny the story of the legacy given to Marcus's brother Frank, but she describes him as 'a gentlemanlike economist, and, as I believe, left no debts.' It is she who provided Linklater with the Gibraltar Jews. It does not make the matter at all forgivable, but it is helpful to know that it was not a pastime reserved for Despards. As Jane writes: 'To torment the Jews at Gibraltar was a daily frolic, and I have heard it cost another officer of the 7th Fusiliers six shillings a week for rotten eggs to pelt the Jews. Dare any officer so amuse himself now-a-days?' I think no comment is needed. The point is that Jane's own stories are the best, such as that of eccentric Despard hospitality:

Many years ago Mrs. Taylor, sister of the present Lord Clancarty, told me that the dearest friend she had was Mrs. Despard of Cranagh, [in Co. Tyrone, Northern Ireland] and her husband was the pleasantest man in the world, but added an expression in a whisper which astonished me "But he was a drunken devil."

Cranagh being divided from the high road by a large lawn he provided himself with a large trumpet, which he sounded to announce dinner to every person going by, as well as to his guests. Indeed I believe in those days travellers were privileged to turn in and dine.

Charity or *bonhomie*? Like her namesake Jane Austen, Jane Despard is observant of rise in fortune and status, and she seems to approve of the Carden genes. Miss Carden was the ancestress of the Donore branch of the family. Sir John Carden, her grandfather, had originally been a butcher in the town of Roscrea. 'Butcher' is rather a wide term. He was a cattle trader and his main fortune came from providing meat to the fleet at Cork. He had the cattle driven to the port, supplying not only the Navy but also the Army in the Peninsular War with salt beef of a high quality. He even exported meat to Bordeaux. As Jane writes: 'He grew so rich that he was said to have found money, and he reared his son a gentleman, whom he then proposed in marriage to Miss Warburton of Garryhinch, one of the thick-blooded antiquities, but not so prosperous. When her father observed "Sir, you have not blood." "No, Sir" said Mr. Carden "but I have fat."'

Jane admits there are weak spots in the family history, 'slippery principles on a sandy soil,' and yet her judgements are mainly positive. She calls George Despard 'one of the excellent of the earth.' Moreover she makes clear that 'None of the Despards of Coolrain were dissipated characters, they were all but one, carefully educated.'

Also she observes 'that the family in general were all temperate and deserve still the appellation of "abstemiousness."' She says that 'The family of Despard were always reckoned particularly clean, not always the case in Ireland.'

However, there was one sad, or rather unfortunate exception to the rule. It must have been her uncle she is thinking of when Jane refers to French history and reflects on the vagaries of fortune, 'so you may see by heads cut off and heads left on there has been notoriety attached to them according as they wagged in wisdom or folly to the right or to the left.' It is as if she sees Edward Marcus doomed from childhood.

Portrait of Edward Marcus Despard painted by George Romney, probably in the 1780s (in the family's possession).

The Colonel

There are only two Despards in standard encyclopaedias. The most famous member of the family was one Jane Despard did not like. As his niece, she saw his profligacy at a very early age:

> The unfortunate Edward Marcus comes next, the youngest and most talented of the whole family. For their knowledge of the Bible and strict morals in their mature and domestic life the elder ones were indebted to a little old grandmother who lived to a great age at Coolrain, and to her private tuition they were obliged to attend during their vacations, but this unhappy man, Edward Marcus, used to detest alike his grandmother, bible and coffee, and to avoid both when he could, dreading the sound 'Master the coffee is ready'.

Even when I was young there was something disreputable about him, almost a family joke. I would show my signet-ring to my friends at school and boast that my ancestor was the last man in England to be hanged, drawn and quartered. Inscribed on the ring was *Pugno*. At St Hilary's school in Sevenoaks we knew perfectly well that meant 'I fight,' but I no idea who had fought for what. The ring bears a dagger and seven drops of blood, one for each conspirator. When I bragged to my friends about this colourful ancestor, was I proud or was I ashamed? It was after all shocking that he should have made an attempt to overthrow Parliament and kill the King. Rather like

Guy Fawkes. There was little sympathy in the family for radicalism and I grew up during the Cold War. Nor was I ever told that he had a black wife.

The first work to appear about Edward Marcus in modern times was *The Unfortunate Colonel Despard and Other Studies* in 1922 by the military historian Sir Charles Oman. In this work Edward Marcus is dismissed as a megalomaniac and as generally cranky. And I think the family were of that mind; at least embarrassed. The historian E.P. Thompson contributed most to the reinstatement of Edward Marcus in his 1963 work *The Making of the English Working Class*. Thompson placed Edward Marcus firmly within the tradition of Thomas Paine's radicalism. When I read this book I became proud of being a relative of the colonel's and I greatly admired Professor Thompson. Years later I was quite close to him; that is, within four feet. It was at an anti-nuclear convention in Finland and E.P. was being escorted by two tall, very earnest campaigners. I didn't dare approach him and it never occurred to me that he might have enjoyed meeting a young woman who knew his book and who bore the name of someone he obviously saw as a hero, one who fought for the Liberty Tree.

Edward Marcus has gone from being anathema to becoming a hero and attracting new biographers. Clifford D. Conner (whose middle initial proves to stand for Despard), author of *Colonel Despard: The Life and Times of an Anglo-Irish Rebel* (2000), and Mike Jay, author of *The Unfortunate Colonel Despard: Hero and Traitor in Britain's First War on Terror* (2004), both gratefully acknowledge Herbert's help in letting them see the family papers. Conner and Jay tell us something about the family in Ireland, though for them all the Georges, Williams and Johns merely form the background to their real story, that of Edward Marcus, the 'unfortunate colonel.'

Edward Marcus Despard was born on 6 March 1751. There was a seventeen-year age difference between him and his oldest brother. In his 1980 book *The Young Nelson in the Americas*, Tom Pocock describes Edward Marcus when he first met Nelson as

> a strikingly handsome man of twenty-eight. Strongly-built, he had the high-mettled looks and scornful lip of the hard-riding country blade that he would have been had he remained in Ireland. Of French Huguenot and Irish blood, he was one of six brothers, of whom the eldest inherited the family seat at Donore, near Mountrath in what was then called Queen's County to the south-west of Dublin, while the others took commissions in the Army. Theirs was a socially well-connected family with a tradition of military service and their prospects were good.

Edward Marcus was executed as a traitor in 1803, having been convicted of leading a plot to overthrow the government and kill George III. He did not start out as a revolutionary, and he was destined to become an officer. Like his brothers, he had an impeccable military career, fighting alongside Nelson in Nicaragua in the war against the Spanish. The purpose of their raid became increasingly obscure and its feasibility more and more impossible in horrible mosquito-infected territory. Yet this is where Edward Marcus proved himself as soldier and engineer. He spoke Spanish and, to judge by the maps he drew up, he was a superb draughtsman. He emerged a hero after the St Juan raid and the assault in 1780 on the Fortress of the Immaculate Conception (El Castillo de la Inmaculada Concepción). He was rewarded with the rank of Lieutenant-Colonel and was made Commander-in-Chief of Roatan, a logging settlement near the mouth of the Black River, Rio Tinto, in present-day Honduras. The small colony was a hotbed of intrigue and indeed this whole chapter is rather murky. Edward Marcus took the part of the freed slaves and the natives – Miskitos of African descent, 'Zambos' or 'Samboes,' as they were called – against the white settlers in their struggle for territory and rights. The white settlers complained and Edward Marcus had to go to London to defend himself. He had private grievances, also to do with money, and by then, I think, larger political concerns. His private grudge had to do with the unfair treatment he had received after his term in Roatan. His political convictions may have been formed in Roatan when he saw how the white settlers behaved. He felt himself unjustly treated and he petitioned without being heard. He was arrested, though as there was no charge he was released after a few weeks. However, on the suspension of habeas corpus, he was once more arrested and spent the years 1792–4 in prison.

In the publication *Public Characters of 1801–1802* the anonymous writer states that he cannot judge Edward Marcus, but he speaks vehemently in his favour. *Public Characters* abhors the treatment he was given in prison: '…when first imprisoned in Cold-Bath-Fields, the treatment experienced by him was cruel in the extreme; and so narrow, it has been said, was his cell, that he was obliged during the rigours of a hard winter, to jump from his table to his bed, and from his bed to the ground, in order to produce such an increased circulation of the blood as could diffuse warmth through his half-frozen veins.'

He was released when habeas corpus was restored, but the writer of *Public Characters* did not know that worse was to come. On his release the colonel became the object of strict surveillance. The spies had reason to be worried; prison had led to further radicalization and Edward Marcus joined the London Corresponding Society. This was an important radical group working for the reform of Parliament and representation by working men. The organization consisted mainly of artisans, and there were many deists in its ranks. Members included Olaudah Equiano, the author and freed slave. Formed in 1792, the society had started modestly and spent five evenings discussing whether they as 'treadesmen, shopkeepers and mechanics' had any right to seek parliamentary reform. Thompson saw Edward Marcus as a central figure in the struggle for parliamentary reform. In these years of the French Revolution, the British government was exceedingly vigilant, imposing harsh restrictions on freedom of expression. Hence the cloak-and-dagger measures Thompson describes:

> A secret committee was meeting in Furnival's Inn Cellar, in Holborn. This was quite possibly a centre of the United Englishmen, an organisation which was in the main an auxiliary to the United Irishmen – indeed in England the two appear almost indistinguishable. Its communications were by word of mouth or by cypher: its emissaries had pass-words and signs: …you reached out your left hand to shake hands with his left hand, then pressing with your Thumb the first joint of the fore finger and he pressing the same with you was a sure token – one saying Unity, the other answering, Truth – one saying Liberty, the other saying Death.

Edward Marcus came more and more to believe in the fight for justice for all. He saw this wider issue linked to the Irish cause. The Society of United Irishmen had been founded in the eighteenth century to work for parliamentary reform. Most of the leaders, including Theobald Wolfe Tone, were Protestants. Protestants had the power because Catholics were barred from the professions and most positions. They were barred by the fact that on taking office they would have had to take an oath of allegiance to the King as head of the Church, which as Catholics they could not do. The aims of the United Irishmen included emancipating and enfranchising Catholics. The organization, inspired by the work of Thomas Paine, looked to America and to France.

The old alliance of Ireland and France was against their common enemy Britain. The Irish movement grew impatient and set a date for a general uprising in May 1798. The United Irishmen were joined by 1,000 French troops, but too late. There were several attempts at a French landing, but all failed, seemingly through a mixture of incompetence and bad weather. The rebellion was severely crushed and in 1801 Ireland became part of the United Kingdom. The Union Jack was complete. This Union has been described as a wedding with the bride raped and her maids of honour drugged.

The United Englishmen formed one of the subservient groups in the wake of the rebellion. To what extent was Edward Marcus involved in the French part of the uprising? According to Conner, 'The lines of communication between United Irish leaders in Dublin and Paris went through London, where Despard served as a liaison.' There is evidence that the maps that were to be used were surveyed by Edward Marcus, which can hardly have helped his case.

Edward Marcus had made a good impression on the diplomat and statesman Talleyrand; when Talleyrand heard he was apprehended he was 'visibly agitated and called the colonel "un homme sur."' However, the French government – that is, Napoleon Bonaparte, the First Consul – was keen to refute any suspicion of being behind a plot to assassinate the King of England. As James Goldsmith, editor of the government-controlled Parisian newspaper the *Argus*, put it, 'All Paris, and the First Consul in particular, learned with horror and indignation, the atrocious attempt which has been made upon the life of his Britannic Majesty, by a desperate Jacobin of the name of Despard.'

Edward Marcus was the only 'gentleman' among the working men he started meeting covertly in taverns, yet he was accepted and liked among the artisans and working men. Francis Place of the London Corresponding Society described him as 'a singularly mild gentlemanly person – a singularly good-hearted man' and 'Orator' Hunt called him 'a mild gentleman-like man.' However, he was conspicuous. The government constraint made it impossible to hold political meetings in public places. He was not belligerent by nature, but he had grown embittered by the way he had been treated and he was caught up in the harsh political climate of the time. The French Revolution was raging a few miles across the Channel and, partly allied to the French, the Irish were trying to free themselves from British rule. It was a time of war and emergency, citizens' rights were waived, and habeas corpus, a writ to prevent people from being unlawfully detained, was suspended. Spies were numerous and in 1802 Edward Marcus and his friends were named by informers and arrested. As a contemporary paper – the *St James's Chronicle* – put it, in true tabloid style: 'The leading feature of the conspiracy is of so shocking a nature that we cannot insert it without pain and horror. The life of our beloved Sovereign, it seems, was to have been attempted by a division of the conspirators, while the remainder were to attack the Tower and other public places.'

Edward Marcus was charged with being the leader of a conspiracy, a group that embraced both Irish and Methodists. Methodism had been started by the fervent Wesley brothers and called for a direct approach to God and a less hierarchical Church. Though Wesleyans started off as social critics they became patriotic and supportive of the establishment as time went on. At this point they were suspect. The writer William Cobbett was both radical and deeply conservative. (One of his strong dislikes was tea.) He was also particularly harsh on Methodists, 'grovelling wretches in and about great towns and manufacturing places,' though it can be said in support of Cobbett that there were many cranky sects at the time, such as 'Ranters,' 'Jumpers,' 'Magic Methodists' and many more. As a deist, Edward Marcus did not deny the existence of a supreme being, but saw no need for organized forms of worship. 'My own mind is my church,' said Thomas Paine, whose works provided reading matter for the colonel. Edward Marcus also asked for a book of mathematics to occupy his brain in prison. He refused attendance of the clergy in prison, even at the very end.

The plot was indeed of a shocking nature. But what *was* it? I have always found it muddling, something about killing the King and stopping the stagecoaches, and I did not see how the two were connected. It seems the plan was to capture the Tower of London and seize the Bank of England. After assassinating the King they would stop the stagecoaches carrying mail, and when this regular service ceased the rest of the country would understand that the insurrection had started. It is not clear how well this plot was thought out, or whether these were the aims. Nor is it clear whether the 'Despard conspiracy' was of the colonel's making. Conner writes that the plot was thought out while he was in prison and that he was not in favour of it. However, he was indispensable to the French because he was educated and they did not judge the labouring classes capable of carrying out anything on their own. The Irish also needed him as they felt he could control the movement and keep it in hand. Conner suggests that his mission was not to provoke a plot, but to prevent it. If Conner's conclusion is correct, the colonel's case is that of a Greek tragedy; he is accused of something he had tried to prevent happening. It was impossible for him to say so at the trial as he would have implicated others.

His trial was a major political event. Lord Nelson was called for the defence: 'We went on the Spanish Main together. We slept many nights together in our clothes upon the ground: we have measured the height of the enemies' wall together. In that period no man could have shown more zealous attachment to his Sovereign and his Country than Colonel Despard.' Despite Nelson's testimony, Edward Marcus was sentenced to be '*hanged, drawn and quartered.*' This was the worst punishment of the law, reserved for high treason. It entailed being 'drawn on a hurdle to the place of your execution, there to be hanged, but not until you are quite dead, then to be cut and your bowels taken out and cast into the fire before your faces: your heads to be taken off and your bodies quartered.' This obsolete punishment was not carried out in its entirety. A public execution was a form of entertainment intended to instil awe into the people and keep the mob in its place. However, this time the authorities feared it might misfire so they dared not display the colonel to the crowd before the execution. They knew he would not be jeered at, and they feared he would be applauded. The hurdle they produced was a cart without wheels to be trundled around the prison courtyard. The colonel himself was unable to keep a straight face at the furtive display of pomp that confronted him. 'Ha! Ha!' he exclaimed with a laugh, 'what nonsensical mummery is this?' The crowd was so great, the atmosphere so inflammatory and so sympathetic to the colonel and his men that there was danger of severe riots. In the end he was hanged with the other prisoners. His end was grisly enough; the executioner who was to cut off his head was unused to the ritual, the axe was not sharp enough and the whole operation was botched. (No wonder the invention of Dr Guillotin across the Channel was considered more humane.)

The behaviour of the condemned was exemplary throughout. His last words to his fellows, when they were putting the noose around his neck, tell us something about his character: 'What an amazing crowd!..'Tis very cold, I think we shall have some rain.' On the scaffold he helped the executioner adjust the noose – in order to break his neck more quickly. John Macnamara is reported to have muttered, 'I am afraid, Colonel, we have got ourselves into a bad situation.' The colonel is said to have replied, 'There are many better, and some worse.' His scaffold speech was carefully weighed, both cautious and full of meaning, hoping that 'the principles of liberty, justice and humanity will triumph over falsehood, despotism and delusion.' It was addressed to his 'Fellow citizens.' The word 'citizen' was in itself delicate at the time of the French Revolution and he risked having his speech abruptly cut off by the platform being dropped.

It is perhaps surprising that *The Times* is restrained in its comments and quotes the whole speech. They must have felt that the crime was so heinous that it spoke for itself. The description is vivid. This worked both ways. The public loved executions and the authorities believed in the spectacle as a form of crime prevention. There was little need to dramatize. The situation spoke for itself:

At four o'clock yesterday morning the drum beat at the horse-guards, as a signal for the cavalry to assemble…..Colonel DESPARD was brought up the last, dressed in boots, a dark-brown great coat, his hair unpowdered…The Colonel ascended the scaffold with great boldness. His countenance underwent not the slightest change, while the awful ceremony of fastening the rope, and placing the cap on his head, was performing. He looked at the multitude assembled with perfect calmness. The Clergyman, who ascended the scaffold after the prisoners were tied up, spoke to him a few words as he passed. – The Colonel bowed, and thanked him…

The ceremony of fastening the prisoners being finished, the Colonel advanced as near as he could to the edge of the scaffold, and made the following speech to the multitude: 'Fellow citizens, I come here, as you see, after having served my country, – faithfully, honourably, and usefully served it, for thirty years and upwards, to suffer death upon a scaffold for a crime of which I protest I am not guilty.'

Thompson concludes: 'When a full view is taken of the evidence, the Despard affair must be seen as an incident of real significance in British political history. It linked the struggles of the Irish nationalists (Despard had some contact with Robert Emmet) with the grievances of London labourers, and of croppers and weavers in the north of England.' From then on writers have seized upon Edward Marcus as a radical icon. I am not quite sure how, but according to the writer David Worrall in his book *Radical Culture* (1992), 'Despard's death was a moment of Foucauldian transition.' Feminist and postcolonialist academics have turned their attention to the colonel's wife, Catherine. He may have met her in Roatan. It has been suggested that she could have been an educated Spanish Creole or the daughter of a Jamaican preacher. Jane Despard was less charitable:

Whether the unfortunate man was ever married to his black housekeeper or not according to his own notions we shall never know, but uncle Andrew, the only one of his brothers who kept up much intercourse with him after his change of politics, seems to think he was not. She was one of a train of black servants he brought over with him and maintained at a hotel in London, for, like his father, he thought his pocket had no bottom.

There is evidence that Catherine Despard was a brave and capable woman whose efforts to save her husband brought her great respect. During her husband's first imprisonment she wrote to the Duke of Portland to ask for an improvement in his condition. She was received by the Duke who summoned the gaoler and gave orders for the colonel to be allowed books and generally be treated according to his rank. Emma Hamilton was a relative of the Despards and was a good friend to Catherine, though this is not the only reason why Nelson spoke on his behalf. Catherine stayed in touch with radicals and smuggled out his writings from the prison in her clothes. She was helped by the radical MP Sir Francis Burdett and was given a pension by him after her husband's death.

The son James E. Despard was not considered part of the family. Jane says he was the son of 'an ensign in the 18th regiment whom my uncle Andrew knew to be born before she and the Colonel ever met.' The verdict of the family was that 'the man who calls himself the Col.'s son has done the family much injury by his bad conduct and gambling character.' Jane reported an anecdote from her earlier years – before the colonel's execution – that his brother General John Despard had told her. The general and two members of his family, 'coming out of the opera house, heard a carriage called for in their name, and there appeared a flashy creole and a flashy young lady on his arm, and they both stepped into it.' This young man may or may not have been Edward Marcus's son. As far as we know we are not in a direct line of descent and the colonel had no other offspring.

What is important to us is the question which also seems to intrigue the historians: how could the rebels Edward Marcus and Charlotte Despard have emerged from such an ultra-conservative background? It must have been tempting for the biographers to make the

Despard family sound as blimpish as possible in order to highlight this paradox. When I was young, people in the family did not hold strong left-wing views and men did not marry black ladies.

Let it be remembered that Edward Marcus Despard was an exemplary officer, but that he lived in a time of war and emergency and that an extraordinary set of circumstances led him to his end.

Charlotte Despard, circa 1910, photographed by Mrs Albert Broom (Christina Livingston). © National Portrait Gallery, London.

Aunt Lottie

Charlotte was no Despard by birth. She was born Charlotte French in 1844, the sister of John 'Jack' French, who was to become Field Marshal French, Earl of Ypres. Though he was to become deeply embarrassed by his sister's radical and Republican politics and activities, there was a close bond between them. They had a difficult childhood. Charlotte and her four sisters did their best to escape supervision, but they were kept from village children. At one point Charlotte ran away from home and took a railway ticket to London where she intended to earn her living 'as a servant.' Their father died when Charlotte was ten and 'Jack' was only two. When Charlotte was sixteen her mother was placed in a home for the 'mentally ill,' having been an invalid for years. Charlotte and her sisters looked after their much younger only brother when he was a child and they later helped him through scrapes and scandals. In his 2011 book *To End All Wars*, Adam Hochschild explores the two opposing strains of belligerence and pacifism during the First World War. A major part of the book is devoted to the brother and sister pair. As a cavalry officer John French was not exemplary (women, drink, debts, more women). Not only Charlotte and her sisters, but also Despard money supported John French in his wild and extravagant younger days. (Perhaps he would make a film hero after all?) And 'Jack' had supported Charlotte. When she made her first public speech at Wandsworth Town Hall in 1891 she was so nervous that her brother had to accompany her to the steps. Like an old soldier comforting a raw recruit under fire, he said, 'Remember, it's only the nervous who are of any real use.'

Charlotte was no conventional beauty. Like George Eliot she had a 'strong' profile. I think this means that she was rather ugly seen from the side, while from the front she was really most attractive. She was tall and thin with a splendid carriage and was most impressive in old age. She took to wearing a mantilla and sandals, but not always; at one point the police were instructed not to arrest any suffragette so dressed. In the well-known photograph of her addressing the crowd in Trafalgar Square late in life she wears large, well-polished men's shoes.

Charlotte married Maximilian Carden Despard in 1870. They were a devoted couple, like-minded, idealistic, full of social concern. They were childless, which was no doubt a great sorrow for them both. Charlotte always loved children. Her husband encouraged her to write novels; I imagine he was stirred by her feminine sensibility and undeterred by the many exclamation marks. Her first novel, *Chaste as Ice, Pure as Snow*, was published in 1874 and others followed. Her books are now reprinted in facsimile, more I presume because of her iconic status than for their literary merit. Her life reads like a novel; her novels do not read like life.

Maximilian died in 1890. After twenty years of marriage and companionship Charlotte was desolate. She thought her life had ended. It had only just begun.

Charlotte Despard is known for her work in several spheres throughout a long life. In brief, she first emerged from her grief by devoting herself to charity. She brought flowers from her beautiful Surrey garden to the poor of Battersea, as some other ladies did. However, she was different; when she saw the appalling poverty and the cruel machinery of the Poor Law, she became radicalized. She went further than the many other charitable ladies and organizations; she went to the root of the problems. From bringing in flowers she ended up by reforming the Poor Law. The Dickensian workhouses were run by Boards of Guardians who administered relief to the poor and needy as they saw fit. She was elected Poor Law Guardian in 1894 and contributed to bringing about the reform of the Poor Law. She worked in Lambeth. (It was while she was guardian that Charlie Chaplin was sent to the workhouse there.)

Social reform led to politics and Charlotte joined the Independent Labour Party. She now unfurled her political energy. It must have been logical for her to turn her energy to the political rights of women, starting as a suffragist and ending up with the Pankhursts and the more militant suffragettes. In 1907 she was twice imprisoned in Holloway, where she was treated with respect. She found Mrs Pankhurst too authoritarian, left her group and became a co-founder of the Women's Freedom League. In 1908 she formed the Irish Women's Franchise League. In 1909 she met Mahatma Gandhi and was convinced by his theory of passive resistance. The campaign for suffrage was suspended when the First World War broke out in 1914. She was an active member of the Battersea Labour Party and was their candidate in the 1918 General Election, receiving only thirty-three per cent of the vote; her pacifism did not make her popular. She moved to Ireland where she and Maud Gonne MacBride worked for Republican prisoners, which again led her to becoming a Sinn Fein activist. In 1930 she visited Russia and was deeply impressed by Soviet Communism. Her enthusiasm did not infect everyone. When she lived with Maud Gonne, it was said that W.B. Yeats took care to visit the house when Mrs Despard was out. She died, rather miserably, in 1939.

Charlotte's Irish Republican zeal was most awkward for her brother John, who had in 1918 been appointed British Viceroy, Lord Lieutenant of Ireland and Supreme Commander of the British Army in Ireland. In 1919 he narrowly escaped being assassinated by the IRA.

Her relevance to this story is that she was married to a Despard and retained a lasting link with the family. We are not quite done with Edward Marcus or with the early family: Margaret Mulvihill, Charlotte's 1989 biographer, makes a point of the radicalism of Edward Marcus, linking it by association to the story of the suffragette. She sees the family as part of the 'benign and deeply civilized Irish Raj,' yet uses the uncomplimentary term 'Horse Protestant' (a term attributed by some to Oliver Cromwell, by others to the Republican writer Brendan Behan). Mulvihill rubs in the Despard/Carden consanguinity, linking this to Charlotte's husband's sickliness as a boy: 'Like many other Anglo-Irish families, they intermarried with their own kind, often with disastrous genetic consequences. No less than three Gertrude Cardens married three George Despards, the last of which marriages produced Maximilian Carden Despard in 1839. Predictably he was a very delicate child…'

Mulvihill points out that the Despard name 'had a particular appeal for the Shelley-besotted rebel' Charlotte. However, it is a far leap from the gruesome end of Edward Marcus to the businessman who married Charlotte. It is said that my father was named in his memory, undoubtedly from affection, and in gratitude of the support he had given my paternal grandfather Bertie in his childhood. However, it can't have missed the notice of my infant father's parents that there might be a massive fortune to inherit from the original, childless Max. Mulvihill writes:

Though not a backwoodsman, grand-nephew Max Despard was no revolutionary. Despite precarious health he made sure he was in the right place at the right time, namely in the Far East in the early 1860s. He went out as the agent of a London shipping firm, and was soon dabbling speculatively on his own behalf in precious stones and the great opium-tea bonanza. China had been 'opened up' to Western exploitation after the first 'Opium War' of 1839–42, in which Britain crushed a Manchu attempt to stop the opium trade in Canton, then the only point of contact between China and Western money. The resulting Treaty of Nanking (which also gave Britain a foothold in Hong Kong) was the first of a series of unequal agreements that legalized the opium trade and granted trade and territorial rights to Western powers. The way was then clear for British businessmen to sell opium produced in India in exchange for Chinese silks, spices and teas. And young Max Despard was in at the killing. […] but life in the East was 'dull' so he concentrated on making his fortune. He was shrewd enough to become a founder investor in the Hong Kong and Shanghai Bank, a decision that would ultimately make his widow a rich woman, and by 1868 he was setting himself up in his own right in London.

More important to us is whether Charlotte's marriage to a Despard was a happy one. Her biographers cast doubt on this. Mulvihill hints that it may have been unconsummated; if so, this would have been due to his poor health. She had apparently confided in her prolific sisters, and at some stage her sister Maggie Jones, not one to mince words, told her granddaughter that Aunt Lottie's Max was 'impotent.'

Circumstantial evidence to doubt the strength of the marriage is that after he died Charlotte did many things Max might not have condoned. What cannot be questioned is the intensity of her mourning.

That Max restrained her impulses may well be so, but it is also likely that grief released unknown qualities in her, which led to enthusiasms that many thought excessive. No one can really know how another person thinks. Even in the most close-knit of marriages the two parties can misjudge each other. A biographer can only judge by what a person says – and this should of course be questioned – by what a person does, their actions also being open to various interpretations, and finally by the reactions of others. That Charlotte wrote many long and slushy novels does not convince us of her good taste. That she sought Max on a Ouija board may equally not convince us of her good sense, but this was a spiritualist quest attempted by many Victorian ladies. Her increasing radicalism must have proved most awkward to the family and it was easy to dismiss her as dotty as she stood haranguing a crowd on the merits of vegetarianism or Soviet Communism.

The following description by Mulvihill is not that of a cranky old woman: 'She proved herself an admirable committee woman, bringing a rare combination of informed compassion, practical experience and military efficiency to the board's deliberations.' What is excellently documented by her biographers is the amount of hard work Charlotte put into each of her causes. Her work in Wandsworth and Nine Elms was impressive. She gave out food and clothing, and boots to barefooted children; she set up clinics and concentrated on the well-being of the underprivileged in every way. She provided mothers with health care, and unlike most charity ladies she made no distinction between married women and common-law wives. She was practical and warm-hearted. In 1891 she bought a house in Nine Elms and set up her first Despard Club. Her clubs gave boys and girls the opportunity to play and read, and kept them off the streets. One of Charles Booth's inspectors was most impressed, investigating 'religious influences' in 1898:

Mrs Despard, a very noble-minded Roman Catholic lady, gives her life to these people, and especially the young among them, and the people recognize her devotion. The boys' club she has made her home: or, perhaps one might better say, her home is their club....She laments the stunted growth of the lads and the early age at which they become their own masters. They are allowed to smoke in the club; it might be better for their growth that they should not, but they will have their 'fags' and it is felt that to forbid smoking would be unwise....In truth the work is ostensibly more social than religious in character, for, though herself a recent convert, Mrs Despard never proselytises, and the representative of the Church of England himself says that if some do adopt her religion it is from admiration of her character.

Charlotte had converted to the Catholic Church. She must have been attracted by its fervency and also it linked her more closely to her new neighbours.

We can be proud of being linked to the Despard Clubs. There are Despard Roads and Despard Streets and a Charlotte Despard Avenue, a tribute to her name. Not many Despards have been teetotal – at least none I have known – but there was at one time, thanks to Charlotte, a teetotal public house in the family name. The Despard Arms was Charlotte's practical way of meeting one kind of wartime distress. According to Linklater, the background for the Despard Arms was that young women, especially soldiers' wives, were turning to the bottle for comfort. They were much despised by the authorities for this; the upper and middle classes having always shown concern for the drinking habits of others. Charlotte pointed out that if women were going to the pubs, it was as much for the company as for the drink and that the only solution was to provide a pub that did not serve alcohol. However, I think the Despard Arms was mainly set up in 1915 to help the women in a different way, by providing friendliness and warmth to their men without the aid of alcohol. The pub must have been for men as it was situated on the Hampstead Road near the big London stations through which troops headed for France. Food and non-alcoholic drinks were served all day and there were baths, cheap overnight accommodation and a club room. The patrons even formed a football club, 'The Despard Uniteds.' At one point Sir John French visited the club and chatted with the men.

I think Charlotte would have liked The Charlotte Despard Pub founded in 2008 on Despard Road off the Archway in the Borough of Islington, London N19, where there is a movie night, a quiz night and a Charlotte Despard blogathon. Last May I made a date with my niece Emma Fischel and my nephew Jonathan Fischel's wife Katie to go there. I had looked forward to making an impressive entrance, ordering a table for Mrs Despard. However, it turned out that they no longer served food. So we parked in the nearby Karl Marx car park, found lunch elsewhere and returned to the pub for coffee. Alas, the opening hours were 4 p.m. till 1 a.m. We ended up rather lamely photographing the pub in the rain. Then we went home.

Charlotte has her own story, lived independently of the Despards, but never quite free from the influence of her husband. Although it was only after the death of her husband in 1890 and after her severe mourning that she devoted herself to the causes for which she is known, she and Max – as she always called him – had shared a streak of idealism. They were firm supporters of Gladstone and Liberal reforms. As Mulvihill says, 'she was a conventionally progressive woman married to a conventionally progressive man.' Her idealism was linked to his. They shared the same eagerness for reform and social justice. The newspaper account of her death states: 'Charlotte French was early imbued with the spirit that was the keynote of her life. In 1870 she married Maximilian Despard, an Irish gentleman who, like herself was trying to discover the causes for the condition of social affairs at that period. Together they interested themselves in sweated labour and the unfair position of women in various spheres.' Max's money lived on for a while, poured into the suffragette movement, vegetarianism, Sinn Fein and Communism, hardly desirable to the Despard family. Yet, as seen above, her sense of social justice and her wish to improve the lot of her fellow citizens cannot be represented in too stark a contrast to the family into which she married. It is too easy to paint a picture of irresponsible and blimpish 'gintry.' My impression of the early Despards and their characteristics as inherited by the first and second Maximilian Carden Despard is that they had a strong sense of social responsibility. They were hard-working, clever, decisive, with practical intelligence and social skills.

Charlotte Despard spent much time on a platform. She was an impressive sight, especially in her old age, tall and thin, a mantilla over her snowy white hair, leaning forward with forefinger raised in admonition or indignation. High-minded people are often better off on platforms than in a drawing-room. However, Charlotte was a great favourite in the family. Her sympathies must have brought embarrassment to many of the 'Castle' Despards, yet there is no doubt that she was close to her husband's family.

'You must read Lucy Franks,' Herbert said. Yet another memoir by a maiden aunt, I thought. But her 1944 typescript was delightful and it also shed new light on Charlotte Despard and how she was loved, especially by the younger generation. Born in 1878, the daughter of Gertrude Despard and Matthew Franks, Lucy was enchanted by her Aunt Lottie and the vision of freedom that was opened up to her. She was not only a devoted admirer as a girl; she remained loyal to Aunt Lottie, even visiting her when she kept vigil for Maud Gonne outside Kilmainham prison in 1923. Lucy was a warm-hearted and valuable chronicler of family life. In her typescript she describes her childhood at Westfield, Queen's County, in Leinster (later Laois).

Lucy's mother Gertrude was the sister of the first Maximilian Carden Despard, and Lucy tells us of the meeting between her uncle and Charlotte French at her parents' wedding. Charlotte and Max spent their honeymoon at the home of the Franks, and Charlotte stayed there many times. Lucy shows how she sowed the seeds of feminism by giving confidence and meaning to the life of a young girl:

> All the Despards clan assembled and a good many of the Franks came from Dublin – the snow was on the ground. Uncle Max was staying at Clondeglas and Mother's chief bridesmaid came from London for the occasion – Charlotte French – witty, clever and enthusiastic, she won Max's affection and they were married some years later. All these facts were told me by Mother when I was a growing girl.
>
> Aunt Lottie had always a devoted admirer in me. She was my play aunt and when she came many were the nursery and school-room regulations I managed to evade with her loving co-operation as she thought I was very much tied down in those days and was not allowed much scope to develop. Life was full of enchantment for me when she came to stay. She opened a new world to me, [one line illegible]... When her handsome husband died on a voyage back from the Canary Islands, where they had gone in a vain attempt to prolong his life, her life seemed to come to a stand still. Insepara-ble companions she sought for some alleviation to her grief. I was fifteen then, and Mother and I crossed to England and went to say with her in her Surrey home near Esher – where she was trying to

adjust her lonely life. Every week she went to London with supplies of flowers from her garden for Lambeth Hospital. Eventually her love of humanity determined her to go and live in a working part of London where she bought up a public house, and established a boys club there, later followed by other activities to which she gave her life, and her charming home at Esher was sold.

The following picture Lucy gives of her grandmother's large family dinners shows a happy family life with no flashes of eccentricity or extravagance. The widow Charlotte left her comforts and entered the world of Oliver Twist; but she had been part of the world of Mr Pickwick. Again I quote in full:

Dinners were plain and heavy in those days, a big boiled cod or haddock – a roast of beef and a couple of chickens – followed by fearful and wonderful "shapes" and jellies! Nothing daunted Grannie, who entertained her family and friends with three old family servants, Graydon from the stables looking very smart, tho the odour of horse still clung to him! Old Mary, prim and protestant and the soul of kindness and stout Mrs. Pigeon who spent her life in the dim, dank basement of the house in E. Fitzwilliam Street, into which shone never a gleam of sunlight and lit by a solitary gas jet when daylight failed. Was it a wonder then that we fished out an occasional hair or feather from our soup plates and even once a cock's leg was brought to light out of the old Sheffield Plate soup tureen to be hastily replaced by my grandmother, but not before the sharp eyes of the grandchildren had espied it! And which gave crows of laughter when related after. One story I remember being told about a Shrove Tuesday dinner party when a big dish of pancakes appeared. Everyone had pancakes and cut lemons until the whole wonderful dish disappeared. An agitated aside from old Mary, the parlour maid, to Grannie – Please Ma-am Cook wants to know who got her wedding ring. Consternation reigns – no-one can produce the ring – no-one found it, several looked uneasy – cook wept and the story finishes that several days after the ring reappeared!

The Franks' house still stands, a good solid house. The tree loved by Lucy is there on the lawn. Ancestors often seem a host of shadowy people, dead and little known by us. We often feel we know fictional characters and film stars better than our own families. And there are undoubtedly many dull ancestors, just as there are dull living relatives. In our family we have the two interesting exceptions Edward Marcus and Charlotte. Yet it takes so little to make those other distant relatives come alive. Lucy Franks does this in the account of her childhood. The young Lucy's thoughtfulness shows the decency of the family, a hunting family like most of their kind in Ireland:

When I was seven I was given a donkey side saddle, having previously ridden in a chair saddle into which I was strapped. When the brothers were all at home from school they had a pony and a couple of donkeys and three or four fox terriers. A list of meets was made out and each day the hunt went out to draw a different covert for rabbits, the old grave yard across a 15 acre field was a favourite draw and many rabbits in and out of the nettles and old graves surrounding the ruins of a little church. In the hunting season we all went out mounted on our different steeds, Harry and George on ponies, Tom on a jennet called Groggy Nick; and I on a donkey – Brandy Bob – both borrowed from local publicans in our village and named in honour! To Johnnie Delaney, one of the farm hands was deputed the honour of attending on me and my donkey with a leading rein – Johnny always arrived clad in his Sunday clothes, and wearing a silver watch, and many a mile did he run with me and the donkey so that I could keep in touch with the hunt.

Two miles away my Godfather, Jack, lived, a great favourite with all the children. To my extreme pride, Johnnie, the donkey and I arrived at Forest with the main body of the hunt. I was invited in to lunch with everyone else and I remember being thrilled at the sight of a huge cheese on the table – I was given a large slice to eat with my bread and butter, when suddenly I had a vision of poor Johnnie waiting with my donkey outside – his dinner hour long past. I stuffed a large piece of bread and butter and half my cheese into the pocket of my riding skirt. Suddenly Godfather Jack saw that my plate was empty – What, have you eaten all that cheese already? I, with flaming cheeks, had to confess I had some in my pocket for Johnnie. I was given more and assured that Johnnie would be well looked after in the kitchen among the grooms. George distinguished himself that day as he appeared in white flannel riding breeches tucked in to his gaiters – these were made from an old pair of cricketing trousers, the flannel being somewhat worn a large hole soon appeared in the seat. Great was the chaffing of all the friends in the field that day on Georgie's hunting breeks!

I don't know whether the children ever asked why the church was ruined or whose graves the rabbits inhabited. There are dark shadows everywhere in Irish history. The horrors of the Famine of 1845–8 were in living memory, and Laois was one of the worst counties to have suffered. However, what this text tells us about our forebears is that they were not grand, but inventive and skilled at making appearances. The stew pot for the poor is not a sign of extravagance.

Not only does Lucy Franks provide an account of Victorian family life and nineteenth-century Despards and Cardens, she also chronicles the direct line from her grandfather to my grandfather, starting with Napoleon and her grandfather George. Lucy's mother was the younger daughter of Captain George Despard of the 43rd Regiment who was one of Napoleon's guards at St Helena in 1816. (He was only sixteen years of age at the time.) He was married young to his cousin, another Gertrude, Gertrude Carden. They had five sons and two daughters and when Lucy's mother (Gertrude) was nine years old her grandfather had a seizure, and died in a few days at the age of forty-three, leaving his widow with a large family and, as he was a younger son, with very little money to educate them. Lucy relates:

The two elder sons William Frederic and George were going through Trinity College at their father's death, for Fred there was an opening found in London, but George – who was studying in the Divinity School – married his cousin Jane Despard of Donore – who was eight years his senior! As he was only 22 and a college student it was rather a case of baby snatching!

There was a third brother, Richard. Now my father's grandfather, my great-grandfather, enters the story. Here are the four generations:

- George Despard (1800–46 – the Napoleon George)
- Richard Carden Despard (1830–63)
- Herbert John Despard (1860–1937)
- Maximilian Carden Despard (1892–1964)

Leading up to Max

Unlike Tristram Shandy my father does not intend to wait until the end of the book to be born. But learning about Max, I felt the need to know more about his immediate antecedents: his grandfather and father and his closest family. One reason why we have so much information about the early family was my grandfather Herbert John's zeal in investigating family history, looking after the papers, typing up Jane Despard's memoirs and keeping family papers intact. A reason for his interest in family may well be that he lost his own father so young and never met his grandfather. There may also have been sadness at no longer being part of the Irish family; he went to Ireland for a wedding once in a while, but that was all. Our direct line of the family left Ireland with Max's grandfather Richard Carden Despard.

At the age of seventeen Richard had to leave Mountrath. His father was dead, his older brothers who had been to Trinity College had inherited, and he had to make his own way. He went to Dublin, booked a berth and arrived in London. He left Ireland on 28 October 1847, moving from the aftermath of the Famine to the railway boom in London. This was a time of dramatic change. The railways transformed society: speeding up industry; transporting goods; allowing people to leave their homes for a cheap fare; bringing physical and social mobility; making fresh food available from the fields to the city markets; spreading newspapers, post and cheap reading matter from the cities to the provinces. When Richard arrived the railways were being constructed and the turbulent growth was visible everywhere with gashes in the landscape, vast cuttings, railway ducts and amazing tunnels. Navvies burrowed in sand and clay, engineers measured, and investors counted their money.

The diary of Richard's first year in London shows that he worked exceedingly hard. He was apprenticed to a firm of surveyors and he worked in the field, surveying with a theodolite and levelling the line which eventually became the southern railway link to Weymouth. He also worked in the office, copying and producing drawings and making statements of accounts. He clearly had the family gift of mathematics and draughtsmanship. By 1858 he was a civil engineer with prospects, but was not prosperous. He seems to embody many of the qualities promoted by Samuel Smiles, such as self-help, self-reliance, frugality and hard work. Smiles celebrated engineers as the greatest heroes of the age. He published his work *Self-Help – with Illustrations of Character and Conduct* in 1859.

'Now you can look at the Hugheses,' Herbert said. Hanging in his stairway were two large paintings I had often walked past but never really looked at. The portraits are rather dark, the faces of the sitters kind, generous. The following correspondence catches the spirit of the Victorian period. John Huntley Hughes, Deputy Lieutenant of Gloucestershire, writes to the young Richard. I don't know if the two correspondents had met before or how Richard met Elisabeth Hughes, but the marriage settlement is the question they are discussing. If there were any Irish recklessness lurking in a corner of Richard, it must surely have been quelled by the sheer benevolence of his future father-in-law, writing on 26 August 1856:

Dear Mr Despard,

True it is, that personally I have known but little of you but still; that little combined with what I have heard from those to whom you are well known leaves me no alternative but to respect your character very highly.

I will not affect to conceal my satisfaction at the prospect of your becoming; in a manner; identified with my family and thereby adding to those members already the object of my satisfaction. Your frank avowal of your circumstances have greatly gratified me; this; my friend is laying the true foundation for the proposed superstructure so long as we are honest and aboveboard we cannot err; how sad it is to be affecting to what we are not – **We are what we are** and let us thank God if in saying so much we can conscientiously lay claim to honesty and uprightness.

I quite agree with you in thinking that we shall better understand each other by personally talking over any little arrangements we may think it right to make. You will find my suggestions as definite as I can make them; but you will always bear in mind that any modification of yours will be favourably considered; I will not presume to offer a[n] opinion as to what you will be able to live respectably upon; one thing only will I venture to caution you against and that is the fatal argument (alas too often used) "We cannot **do** with **less** than so and so, and let me tell you more, if we are wise we can do with even less than that.

It is our duty to circumscribe our expenses (be our income what it may be; great or small) as to leave us with a surplus account wherewith we may befriend those whom we love and may require our assistance and my firm belief is that God will help us if we conscientiously use the gifts of his providence and that for their abuse He will call us to account on the last great day.

Richard replies in the same vein, though more modestly:

Dear Mr Hughes,

How can I thank you sufficiently for your kindness? Indeed I feel humbled and abashed when I hear of the good opinion entertained of me, and feel how very little it is deserved.

For our especial reason however I cannot but feel rejoiced and trust it will be of great advantage to me – namely because it will be an additional incentive "to keep me up to the mark" – and God helping me I hope I may be enabled to do so.

In the very kind advice you have given me, I most sincerely thank you and assure you, it is most highly valued by me, and in every word you have written I entirely and cordially agree. It shall indeed be always my earnest endeavour to act in accordance with it, and I do hope and trust that whenever you see reason and feel dissatisfied with any of my proceedings you will kindly and candidly inform me. As no other proof of your regard could be most gratifying.

This correspondence seems to have taken place eons ago, but genetically the link is very short. Richard was my great-grandfather. I know children who have perfectly intact great-grandfathers and many people I know are themselves great-grandparents. The marriage to my great-grandmother, Elisabeth Huntley of Torquay, aged twenty-two, took place on 11 August 1857. They had two children: Louise, known as 'Louie,' and her brother Herbert John, born on 1 February 1860. Three years later, on 18 March 1863, Richard died. Thus Herbert John, my grandfather, was left without a father at the age of three. He was orphaned at thirteen, when Elisabeth died in 1873, after which the children were looked after by their maternal grandparents, the excellent Hughes, and by Uncle Max and Aunt

Lottie. Charlotte outlived Max and always wrote to her 'beloved Bertie,' 'her dear dear Bertie.' Louie, by then Mrs L.G. Davies, died in 1929. Lucy Franks attended her funeral.

When I was thirteen I received an official-looking letter in the post. It was exciting; rather like something in an Enid Blyton book. I had inherited £1,000 from a distant relative. It was a big event. I had to take a bus to Sevenoaks and a train to Tunbridge Wells where I had an appointment with the friendly bank manager. I was ushered into his office and then taken to a counter where the mysteries of the cheque-book and my account were explained. My brother-in-law had told me about interest and how it could 'accrue.' I liked that word, now that I was a rich young woman. I had never heard of my relative, Colonel Despard Davies, and only now have I understood that he was my father's cousin, the son of Louie. I wish we had met.

Herbert John and Beatrice Lorne, circa 1920.

Parents

'There has never been an ugly Despard.'

These were the words of my Aunt Margery. Certainly her step-father, Max's father, was known as 'the Beautiful Bertie.' So where did his good looks come from? And Max's height? All Jane Despard tells us is that the Despards had 'black hair and white teeth.' Margery was not a great beauty, but she was attractive. She was short, half the size of Max. She always wore very short skirts. Aunt Margery was not a Despard herself but the half-sister of Max, daughter of Beatrice Lorne and Major Roger Dennistoun.

Her stepfather Herbert John Despard was trained as a soldier. He was a captain of the Royal Scots Fusiliers and the West India Regiment. He served as a young officer in South Africa from 1880–1 and was mentioned in despatches. He took part in the defence of Rustenburg. The First Boer War was not a time of glory for the British. It also marks the end of one type of warfare and heralds a new way of combat. The Boers were farmers and hunters, excellent marksmen. They knew they had to strike with the first shot and that if they reloaded the game would be far away. They blended into the terrain in their drab farming clothes, whereas the British troops still wore red jackets and blue trousers.

When Herbert John was seconded to the West India Regiment he met Beatrice Lorne Dennistoun, a widow with one daughter, Margery. Beatrice's maiden name was Jarvis and she was born in

Antigua. The family's sugar plantations of up to a thousand acres were run from the family mansion and prospered hugely. The Jarvis family seem to have been responsible citizens, though they made their fortunes before the abolition of slavery. In Antigua the plantation owners were largely resident, which was not always the case elsewhere in the Caribbean. Their fortunes increased in the nineteenth century and Beatrice was no doubt a wealthy young woman. Mount Jarvis was named after the family.

I did find a very private glimpse into the lives of our grandparents. Bertie courted Beatrice in verse in tiny writing:

To Lorne
    Leave destiny to the greater powers above
    Only learn this dear, that you're made for love
    Remembering that for me there's no night nor morn
    Nor happy thoughts; when you from me are torn
    Evening and gloom set in, – and then I die for-Lorne.

    I've been perpetrating nonsense in a sort of rhythmic fashion
    And making almost public a most absorbing passion
    It means just what in fancy, you may like to make it mean
    Nothing more or less. – But its not intended to be seen.

In 1890 they married. Beatrice had money of her own and was a capable woman in her own right. During the Great War she obtained an OBE for her war work. She wore dresses down to her ankles and was a very handsome woman – indeed she looked rather like Bertie, according to Anita and Herbert. They remember her as a great card-player who taught them to play poker and whist. In the winter Herbert John and Beatrice would go to Menton for his health as he suffered from asthma and emphysema. While there she went to the casino. Her bookmaker knew her as 'Dolly Daydreams.' She had no need to play for winnings. When she died in 1934 she left over £16,000 tied up in shares for Blantyre Gas, the Volga Steamship Co. Ltd, Burmah Oil, the British South Africa Co. and British Government War Stock, as well as jewellery worth £1,253 and furs worth £182.

We know a lot more about Herbert John than we do about his wife, as all his testimonials were printed up and there were also newspaper cuttings in the 'MAX' box. When he married he gave up his commission and set out to be a chief constable. He had a good head for the law and in 1893 was appointed Chief Constable of Dewsbury. After that he applied for the position of Chief Constable of Hereford. In the small booklet of his applications and collected testimonials he stated that he was thirty-five years of age, 5 ft 10 1/2 in. tall and married, and that before joining the police service he had gained considerable experience 'in the conduct of prosecution and the preparation of evidence, and in the duties of the Military when called out in aid of the Civil Power in times of disturbance.' He submits the testimonial that E.T. Bainbridge, a colonel in the Royal Scots Fusiliers, had written when he applied for a prison appointment two years previously. The colonel gives a pleasant description of his character and personality: 'Now, in an appointment in the Prison Department, a nice manner in dealing with those under you – also good tact and judgment are essential – and these are qualities in your character which I have always remarked when you were my Adjutant.' T. Bateman, Alderman and JP for the Borough of Dewsbury, writes that Herbert John was 'smart, straight and reliable, kind to the men and liked by them; he has their confidence and the confidence of the Magistrates before whom he conducts his cases with credit, fairness, and discretion.'

It was an achievement to have been appointed Chief Constable of Lanarkshire at the age of thirty-six. Among his duties was 'the supervision of music and dancing licenses, &c., and also of traction engines.' But more serious matters had tested his worth. Frederick Ellis, Justice of the Peace acting in and for the West Riding of Yorkshire, regrets that he might move to another post: 'I can say from my own personal knowledge that he is a most able and efficient officer. I had exceptional opportunity of judging of his qualifications during the very sad and serious disturbances which took place in this district during the late Coal Strike.' It is unclear which these particular 'disturbances' were. However, there was at the time a good deal of social unrest, not least due to the struggle of the newly founded Miners' Union for better working conditions.

Herbert John was not afraid of making decisions and one of his most controversial acts concerned the Irish July marches that also took place in Scotland. Every 12 July the Orange Order marched in their regalia to commemorate the Protestant victory at the Battle of the Boyne in 1690. In Shotts on 12 July 1905 Captain Herbert John Despard called out the police, intervened, and arrested Orange bandsmen for playing tunes he knew could cause trouble, even violence. He and Alexander Andersen, superintendent of the police, were then sued by David Carson, a miner, and secretary of one of the bands, for '£100 damages each for alleged wrongous apprehension.' The case was widely followed by the press. Every 12 July there had been disturbances, this year in many other places, and there was an added threat that an attempt might be made to wreck the new Roman Catholic church at Shotts. Captain Despard received a worried telephone call from Father Scanell at Mossend that the Orangemen were going to march through that area and that the Catholics would not tolerate any insults.

Herbert John's testimony at the trial is quoted at length by the press: 'Witness [i.e. Captain Despard] understood that they were not going to tolerate any tunes like "Kick the Pope" being played outside the church.' Herbert John had also argued that the wearing of swords by the Orangemen was an added provocation. His motive in preventing the Orange tunes being played was 'to protect the Orange band from being assaulted and injured by the Roman Catholics if they played the tunes. He had not the slightest ill will towards the Orangemen.' 'Knowing Irishmen as he did, he knew they were playing these party tunes to irritate the Catholics.' 'Witness was neither a Roman Catholic nor an Orangeman.' He maintained that it was a crime for a band to play to insult people, just as much as it would for a Protestant to stand in his door and say 'To hell with the Pope' as Roman Catholics were passing.

A Glasgow newspaper reports that the court was asked by the judge to decide whether Captain Despard had acted 'maliciously and without probable cause.' Thus thrown on its common sense the jury had no difficulty in deciding that 'Captain Despard had acted legitimately in view of the circumstances, and that verdict will be hailed with general satisfaction throughout the West of Scotland.' The trial had a sequel. In June 1906 the Court of Session set the seal of illegality on the public playing of party tunes. The case is interesting because the tunes are still being played, even louder. Also it shows Herbert John's integrity and judiciousness.

My grandfather received the OBE, mainly for his superb organization of the royal visit to Lanarkshire in July 1914. He was hailed as Chief Organizer of the Triumph, and indeed the programme had been planned minute by minute. Their Majesties King George V and Queen Mary were conveyed with military precision from railway station to factory to luncheon and function. In 1920 Herbert John received a letter informing him that 'in view of the service you have rendered on work connected with the War, it is proposed to submit your name to the King for appointment as a Commander of the Order of the British Empire (Civil Division).' His war work was for the families and bereaved of servicemen as Honorary Secretary of S. & S. Families Association, Lanarkshire.

When Herbert John was appointed Chief Constable of Hamilton, Lanarkshire, it was to his advantage that his stepdaughter Margery married Mr Roger Poore, whose sister had married the Duke of Hamilton. Not least it provided him with good shooting. Max remembered standing at the back of the line in a cloud of smoke from the cartridges. This elevates the family to a certain extent. It also brings us closer to the coal mines that were to benefit the family later.

Herbert John had proved himself an impartial upholder of the peace in the Orange case of 1905. We can only wonder how he reacted to the following letter from his Aunt Lottie, written in Dublin on 18 December 1921, recently found among family papers and not previously published. Charlotte Despard never failed to keep in touch with her family. These family letters are affectionate and do their best to impart her enthusiasm for her causes. Her political sentiments cannot have been music to the ear of the Chief Constable of Lanarkshire, but I love the way she addresses him as if they were like-minded in all things. The letter heading is 'Votes for Women,' but her main cause now in the midst of the terrible Troubles of the early 1920s is that of Irish nationalism:

My dear old Bertie

Indeed, indeed I have not forgotten you or dear Lorne or the days that have been and I reproach myself for not having written sooner to tell you of the change in my life. To many it may seem strange that at such an age as mine, one should pull up the stakes and more or less break with the past; but that is what I have done. For some time past I have been, in my way, through voice and pen fighting for Irish Liberty in England and last year exposing to the world the atrocious cruelties that were being perpetrated here. Early this year it came to me that I would have to do more. I determined then to take up my Irish nationality, move over here and do what I could to help our people in their sorrow. From February until late October I lodged and boarded with Maud Gonne MacBride who has been for some time a dear friend of mine. Now, at last, I have succeeded in getting a house of my own. I have bought the place at a wonderful bargain – a large old-fashioned house in a beautiful garden and I am carrying out a plan which has long been in my mind, to bring in for comfort, rest and healing some of those who have suffered in these terrible times. I have now a family – mother and five children, who had their house in Belfast fired by an Orange mob. The father – a Catholic and a most respectable man is trying to get work in Dublin. I expect also in a few days to receive prisoners – I cannot tell you all I am doing. This is just to give you an idea of why I am here. My house in Nine Elms I am giving over to the Battersea Borough Council for the benefit of the people amongst whom I lived so long.

Now, this is my news. I may not live much longer though I am quite well now; but, if I do live, I should love to see you and Lorne over here.

My dear fellow, we Sinn Feiners have neither class nor religious differences and we do not allow our priests to dictate to us politically. Amongst us there are many Protestants – and these are not the least keen for liberty. So come over some day and see us.

I am much interested with your news – especially to hear that you are a grandfather in your own right – you who like me never intend to grow old. May every blessing be on the head of the youngster [Terence]! And dear Lorne – it is good to hear that she is stronger.

Ireland is not going to disappear, dear boy! A new Ireland is arising. A thousand years ago this little island of the West was the light of the world. She will be so again.

My very true [not legible] love and best Christmas wishes to you all –special love to yourself and Lorne

Your affectionate Aunt

C. Despard

Charlotte was in her seventies and would live for another twenty years. In 1920 she was a mourner at the death of Terence MacSwiney, the Lord Mayor of Cork, following his two-month hunger strike. She was also appalled at the hanging of 18-year-old Kevin Barry in Dublin that same year. She had joined the Republican ranks.

Herbert John died in Sidmouth in 1937. We have no mention of it other than his obituary in the shorthand reserved for that column of *The Times*:

DESPARD, *Capt.* Herbert John, C.B.E., son of the late Richard Carden Despard; *b.* 1860; ed. At King's Coll., London, and at R.M.C.; Capt.Roy. Scots Fusiliers and West India Regt., and a D.L. for Lanarkshire; S.Africa 1880–81(despatches); Ch. Constable, Dewsbury 1893–96, since when of Lanarkshire: *m.* 1890, Beatrice Lorne, O.B.E., da. of Thomas Jarvis, of Mount Jarvis, Antigua, and widow of major R.J.W. Dennistoun, N. Staffordshire Regt: *cr.* C.B.E. (Civil) 1920. *Balgreen, Hamilton, Lanarkshire: Naval and Military Club.*

Brothers and Sisters

Herbert John and Beatrice Lorne had four children. Herbert Leslie (Tommy) was born in 1891, Max a year later. Herbert John's only daughter, Beatrice Ierne, was born in 1895. Then in 1896 Geoffrey Edward Patrick was born.

Margery was not Bertie's child, but she was the only one I knew. I knew she had a sad past, but was never aware that she had lost her first child Lorne Heather, who was born on 23 December 1914 and died on 22 February 1915. Lorne Margery was left a widow young. Major R.A. Poore was killed in action in September 1917 commanding the 2nd Battalion Royal Welsh Fusiliers. She was left with a son, Roger Dennistoun, known as Dennis, who was born on 19 August 1916. Both world wars affected her sorely. She lived in Ferneyhurst, a house with spacious grounds not far from Southampton. I can remember the forest of dark and forbidding rhododendrons. Max stayed there in the 1930s when he was home on leave. In the Second World War the house was full of refugees from Portsmouth, mainly children. A bomb fell on the middle of the house and when Margery opened her bedroom door, she found a void. Many of the children had been killed. The house was somehow patched up and she went on living there with Aberg, her chauffeur, and Mrs Aberg, her maid. In her stables stood, perfectly kept, the Argyll car in which she had left for her honeymoon. The car survived Margery and now has pride of place in the Beaulieu

Tommy and Max in kilts in Hamilton, circa 1900.

Motor Museum. There was a voice pipe between the chauffeur and the back of the car and Aunt Margery said that if you blew hard enough you could blow off his hat.

We were very fond of Aunt Margery with the short skirts, and to many of us younger members of the family she was our one link to the past. Her class consciousness remained unscathed. 'The miners sang as they went to work.' 'The working classes do not know what to do with themselves on holiday in Spain.' And 'What will you do for servants?' on my sister's marriage in 1952. She was a great reader. She sat in her 'boudoir' overlooking the garden. One of the rooms in her house was devoted to jigsaw puzzles. In that room the pictures were hung so high that no one could really see them, but the outstanding feature of the jigsaw room was a Pianola into which one put rolls of music. You had to pedal to make it work and this was quite strenuous for Aunt Margery as she was so short.

Many of the cars were driven by Dennis. He took a degree in Engineering, and became a well-known racing driver (even completing a race after being stung by a wasp). He had a successful career in the City. My cousin Dennis was rich, intelligent and capable. When I lived with my sister and all her children in Kent we loved his visits. He would arrive in a camel-hair coat in a large car. At teatime he would grab huge slices of bread distractedly while reading *Girl Annual*.

I did meet Tommy, my father's oldest brother, once. The following is as much as I know of him, the eldest but not the most illustrious of John Herbert's sons. He got his Wings during the Great War, having first reached the rank of Captain in the Army. (The Royal Flying Corps, or RFC, was the air arm of the British Army during the First World War until it merged with the Royal Naval Air Service in 1918 to form the Royal Air Force.) The pacifist Charlotte does not hesitate to approach her brother, Sir John French, Field Marshal, to help Bertie obtain a position for his son Tommy in Egypt. Again we see that Charlotte does not fail to mention the Irish cause or Socialism in her letters to the chief constable. She writes from Sussex, 9 August 1917:

My dear old Bertie,

(I did not write at once on receipt of your letter, for I was in the throes of our summer-move, but I did what I hope is better. I sent [illegible] with a line from myself to my brother and I have had an answer from him this morning. The Sirdar, he says, is an old friend of his. He is writing to him; but we must understand – as of course, we do – that all are judged on "their own merits". I do hope your boy will have his wish. [...]

I am busy, as usual, amongst my labour-movement friends. I do so earnestly hope that they will now, at last, show themselves united and strong. The war and its results have opened many eyes.

Kindest love to you and yours

Always your affectionately

C. Despard

I think of a Sirdar as some exotic potentate draped in robes, but it was the rank assigned to the British Commander-in-Chief of the Egyptian Army. Tommy was appointed, served in Egypt, and after the Armistice returned to Britain looking for a job. He went to Malaya as a rubber-planter and became manager for the Dunlop Rubber Company, first at Batang Melaka in Malacca, and then in Johore. From his letters we see that he enjoyed life as a planter. The *Singapore Free Press and Mercantile Advertiser* and the *Straits Times* also give regular accounts of the cricket matches where he scored well, frequently captaining the Genuang Cricket Club. He married Maud, a nursing sister (Telegram to his father: GOT MARRIED STOP SEND

MONEY.) However, there is a bleaker notice in the *Singapore Free Press and Mercantile Advertiser* on 17 May 1926: 'DESPARD. April 14, at 27, at 27 Welbeck Street, W.I, to Maud, wife of Herbert Leslie Despard, of Seremban, daughter, stillborn.'

After Maud's death he married her sister Edith Annie. When the Japanese attacked Singapore she was evacuated on the SS *Duchess of Bedford*, arriving in Liverpool on 4 April 1942. She was thirty-four years old. Tommy was fifty-one, but volunteered for the defence and was captured by the Japanese. He was imprisoned with some 4,700 others at the Changi Jail, built to house around six hundred. He is registered as a planter and civilian internee in the 1942 Changi register with spouse Mrs E.A. Despard, c/o Chartered Bank, London. In 1944 prisoners were transferred to the Sime Road camp. This was originally a British Operational Headquarters, but when the Japanese had swept through the country it became an internment camp holding mainly British and European civilians. However, by the end of the war there were 4,507 persons from twenty-seven nationalities in the camp, including over a thousand women and some three hundred children. These were perhaps not the cruellest of the Japanese camps, but dysentery was rife and there were many deaths. A tall man, on his release Tommy weighed eight stone, or just over 50 kg. He was repatriated, arriving in Liverpool on 8 October 1945. While investigating his pension he discovered that Dunlop had deducted the years in prison from his years in active service to the company. He died in 1971. His son, John, was by all accounts an equally keen cricketer.

I did not know Ierne, though I think we once went to see her in her house in Scotland. Ierne was always called 'the Rabbit.' Anita suggests that she may have had the same habit as Max. He twitched his upper lip and nose when thinking, and the children said, 'Daddy, you're rabbiting again.' Ierne did not have sticking out teeth or other herbivore features. Indeed she was an attractive young woman, though perhaps not as pretty as her friend Nora Moore. In 1923 she married Donald Grant who had served and was gassed in the Great War. Their children were Geoffrey and Jill. Geoffrey died in 1945 when crossing the Rhine as a glider pilot. His twins were born posthumously. When Beatrice became a widow she lived with Ierne. According to Herbert, Ierne was an efficient woman who ran a good house and baked her own bread. Ierne's husband Donald Grant was very small, and Max said that when they travelled they put Donald in the luggage rack.

I had never heard of my uncle Geoffrey until I was working on this book. He died young and was little talked of. I didn't even know he had existed. He clearly did well in his short life and I think he deserves more than a passing mention. He had a weak heart, which was discovered at his medical examination for military service, so in the First World War he was passed for home service only. He became a recruiting officer based in London. This was to me an unknown and interesting side of the war. It was no sinecure. On the outbreak of war in August 1914 the response was overwhelming. Parliament called for 500,000 soldiers, but over 750,000 men had enlisted, and by January 1915 a million. However, two in five volunteers were discovered to be entirely unsuitable on health grounds. The enlistment had to be organized. Lord Derby then had the idea of 'Pals battalions,' groups of men from the same workplace, village, bank or football team joining up together. This was seen as positive then, but was abandoned later as heavy casualties in one such battalion could be devastating for a small community. There was set a time limit to the possibility of enlisting under this scheme, which increased the pressure of the

Ierne, 1914.

work for Geoffrey. A newspaper reports: 'Last Thursday was the day that saw the beginning of the GREAT RUSH that tried the energy and patience of the recruiting officers, Major F. Cannon and Lieut. Despard, with their able and sacrificing staff. In spite of all trials the recruiting officers were courteous, helpful and considerate – the qualities of gentlemen.'

There were medical reports to be made as well as an assessment of how fit the men were for military service and how motivated. Geoffrey worked at East Ham Town Hall, which was besieged by volunteers, with police controlling the crowds and a concert arranged upstairs to distract those who were waiting. The doctors worked at full speed but could barely keep up with the demand. And then there was a day's pay to be handed out. The climax for the men came when 'in absolute silence Lieut. Despard swore in a batch of 500 men, giving a thorough explanation, and informing them all that they were soldiers.' This day's work was not enough. From another newspaper clipping:

After dealing with hundreds of men on Thursday, the recruiting officers were nonplussed what to do with the crowds of men that again presented themselves at the Town hall at eight o'clock in the morning, before the offices opened. The large number of men who turned up last evening were sworn in batches without being medically examined, and without receiving pay. One man who arrived at the Town hall at 8.30 in the morning was not sworn in until 5.15 in the evening. During the day Lieutenant Despard visited Stirling's telephone and electrical works at Dagenham, and attested 102 men. In the early hours of this morning he will again visit the works to swear in the night shift.

Another tribute to a young man:

> Major Cannon, the chief recruiting officer for East Ham, was the first to recognise the invaluable services rendered by his second in command Lieut. Despard, to whose extraordinary efforts the success of recruiting in East Ham, under Lord Derby's scheme, was very largely due. The Major himself has been unremitting in his attendance and supervision, but he was fortunate in having so energetic and diplomatic an assistant as the lieutenant. Not even a navvy could say that he was not treated with courtesy and consideration at the hands of the lieutenant. The work did not consist merely of swearing in recruits, but entailed innumerable enquiries and much correspondence, which tired even the robust energies of Lieut. Despard to their utmost. For nearly three days he was denied his bed, but under all the stress his good humour and suavity never failed, and all who worked with him are loud in their praise of his work.

Geoffrey died on 17 March 1921. His death is not mentioned in the letters we have. His parents had proudly kept the newspaper clippings, but they must have kept their mourning letters separate. I have no photograph of him.

Max aged six in Hamilton, 1898.

'A lote of boys'

Maximilian Carden Despard, second son of Herbert John and Beatrice Lorne, was born in Heaton Norris, Stockport on 30 March 1892. I cannot remember anything my father told me about his childhood and youth, other than that he saw Queen Victoria's funeral procession. After over a century Max is no longer 'remembered as the desperado son of a distinguished Chief Constable.' However, Aunt Margery would hint at a healthy and energetic youth in Scotland: 'We would bicycle ten miles to play tennis.'

Max was not the oldest nor the youngest of the children, but I suspect he was his parents' golden boy. He had faith in his ability; he worked hard and set out to fulfil his ambitions. Even if we do not know what pranks the boys got up to at home, or anything at all about their childhood, we can see from his letters that Max took school seriously. He and his brother Tommy were sent very young to Stubbington House in Fareham, Hampshire. It is difficult to decipher the year from the postmark, but we do have one of the first letters he wrote from school to his mother:

The Headmaster's wife writes to reassure Beatrice that Max and Tommy are keeping well:

Dear Mrs Despard
    Your two little men are settling down most happily to school

life. I have not seen even a look of sadness as yet. Both tell me that they are getting on very well in every way, and are quite comfortable. They seem exceedingly nice little boys, and I feel sure will become general favourites in the school. A report on the work will be sent to you soon. Yours sincerely …

P.S. I think they have everything they require, and subscriptions are added to the accounts. They are having 4D per week pocket-money each.

By the time Max was twelve years old there were serious matters to consider. He was to take the train to London – First Class, naturally – to sit for an entry exam to the Royal Naval College, Osborne, on the Isle of Wight. A good question is why Max, from an Army family, should choose the Navy. The answer is to be found in the school.

In the nineteenth century, nepotism was giving way to meritocracy. One way of ensuring that the best men occupied the best positions was the introduction of entrance exams: to the Civil Service in 1855 and to the Royal Navy in 1838. The result of this was the growth of both public and preparatory schools to enable boys to pass the exams. Stubbington House, just across the Solent from Osborne, was one such school. 'No school had stronger ties with the Royal Navy in the nineteenth century than Stubbington House,' it has been said. So, despite his family's military background, there was no question of Max's future career and his choice was made at an early stage. In 1904 he writes from Stubbington House to his mother:

Thank you very much for the time table, but Mr Isaacs [?] gave me one before, he has settled all about the….after the exams on Thursday. There is a match today against the Portland Beugles [Bugles?

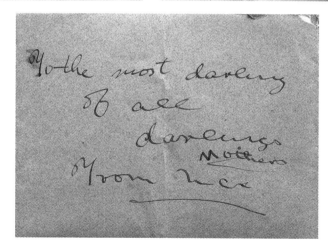

May 3st

my Dear Mother
I like the school
very much.
thire are such
a lote of boys
thank you
awuly much
it such a big
place thire is a
large choieet
field. and I was
playing yestarda
with some other

boys. all the
boys rite letters
on saerday
all the nastem
wear foter.
photographede
- from your
loving mad
Max

To the most darling
of all
darlings
Mother
from Max

On the back of the envelope Max writes, 'Do not send it away to somebody else'.

Beagles?] here, we have got a few masters playing, there are over 64 boys on the sick-list with cold's, I have still got one. During the exams we stay at the "Golden X Hotel" quite close to the Medical Hall, were the exams are held.

Then he writes rather grandly from the Golden Cross Hotel, Charing Cross to tell his mother: 'I passed my medical all right this morning. But now it is the evening of the 6th. The exams were rather easy today. I think I have done rather well. We have French conversation tomorrow (Oral Examination). I will see you on Thurs-day (most probably).'

He had reason to be confident. On 21 December 1904 a telegram was handed in at the Admiralty, London addressed to Captain Despard, Chief Constable, Lanark: HAD TO SAY YOUR SON MAXIMILIAN WILL RECEIVE A NOMINATION UNDER THE NEW SCHEME.

On 22 December 1904 the Admiralty sends a letter to Mr Maximilian C. Despard – aged twelve: 'SIR, I am commanded by My Lords Commissioners of the Admiralty to acquaint you that, having passed successfully at the recent examination for Naval Cadetship, you are hereby appointed to H.M.S. "RACER" for the Royal Naval College, Osborne, from the 15th January 1905.'

Naval College

At some point in his life Max was provided with a horoscope. Where or how he got it, I do not know. It seems uncharacteristic, but he kept it. Here are some of its findings:

– You are a born leader and must be at the head of everything. You are not a good servant and are at your best when you can plan and scheme…. You are enthusiastic, impetuous and self willed…

– You love comfort and delight in taking life easily. You are possessed of great personal charm but can be very obstinate.

– You are possessed of energy courage and powers of endurance.

– You will be very popular. You will attract powerful friends who will be ready to help you. Your success will depend on the amount of work you put in as the influence of Jupiter is towards a lackadaisical tendency.

– You have an excitable disposition and are prone to take risks and court danger. In fact you delight in taking chances. You will also be a person quick to make decisions whether they are right or wrong. You will not therefore always weigh up the pros and cons sufficiently and may often make wrong decisions.

A leader of men, ambitious and energetic; this was Max. No one is born an officer; the qualities and skills are instilled through training. No one is born a leader of men; latent qualities of leadership only emerge when

Max as a Navy cadet, probably in 1905.

tested, and are strengthened with the practice of command. The values imparted at the turn of the last century were qualities that would take the young men through two world wars.

Max was enrolled at the Royal Naval College, Osborne in May 1905. Osborne had been the summer residence of Queen Victoria, built for her by Prince Albert in 1840. After the Queen's death in 1901 the house was bequeathed to the nation. This was perhaps not such a very magnanimous bequest as apparently Bertie, now Edward VII, had never liked the place and the Royal family thought it a white elephant. The estate became a junior officer training college for the Royal Navy. This training had previously been carried out on ships in the River Dart in Devon. Dartmouth College was also fairly newly established at the time Max enrolled. Osborne was not without teething difficulties: there were several cases of rheumatic fever, and one of its famous alumni, Jack Llewelyn Davies, described his five years there as 'horrendous.' As he was one of the brothers who inspired J.M. Barrie this is not altogether surprising; it was perhaps not the place for Peter Pan. My father seems to have enjoyed himself there; at least, we have never heard anything to the contrary.

The college aimed to complete the boys' general education. It differed from public schools in being 'more modern and less classical.' The aim was to introduce them

> to the fascinating science and art of the seaman, and by this I mean all branches of seamanship, navigation, the handling of sailing craft, knowledge of winds and currents, the art of pilotage, ship husbandry, and all the multifarious duties which form the day to day life of the sailor, be he in the Royal Navy or in the Mercantile Marine.

They were to study the 'science and art of war,' in theory and in practice through a thorough technical education which included the handling of weapons. The course of study included the following subjects: Mathematics, with geometrical Drawing; Physics and Mechanics, with laboratory work; Engineering, with workshop practice and Mechanical Drawing; Seamanship; Navigation; French, with German later; English Grammar and Composition; English Literature; History, including Naval History; Geography; Bible Study; Drill. A large proportion of the time of the cadets was 'given to the practical study of Engineering in Workshop and Instructional Steamboats attached to the College.' It seems as if it was a good and sensible education, a fine blend of theory and practice. It is as if I can see those uniformed boys of various sizes memorizing parts of speech and parts of guns. There is a surprising emphasis on the humanities, yet the most important quality to be instilled was that of leadership.

Leadership means being able to take on responsibility. In an address to the boys at the beginning of their course – an education that was to take them from being schoolboys to naval officers – they were told, 'Do not be afraid of accepting responsibility, nay, seek it wherever you can find it in your early days, grasp it with both hands, so that in later life, when it is thrust upon you, your shoulders will bear it without strain.' To be a leader, you must know how to be led. The address was given many years before the two world wars, but it is made clear that the British knew the true value of leadership, as opposed to the Germans, who imposed blind discipline: 'The Germans aim at such discipline that unquestioned obedience will be enacted irrespective of the qualities of the officer. In the British system, the essentially British compromise of a happy mean, is adopted. High qualities of leadership [are] expected of the officer, whilst discipline, though sound, is more flexible than that of the Germans.'

Max may well have remembered the gist of this speech when faced with his biggest challenge, the action on the *Broke* in 1917. Teddy Evans's

Max with Parnell and other midshipmen, circa 1912. They all enjoyed coaling when both men and officers were covered in coal dust.

perfect leadership consisted in planning so well that each and every man knew what to do. Before the battle one single order was issued.

The ships drawings made by Max show his skill and the high level of work expected. In November 1908 'The Royal Life Saving Society, The Elementary Certificate' was awarded to 'Maximillian [*sic*] Despard, Royal Naval College for passing the elementary tests of the Society in Swimming Object Diving Life Saving and Resuscitation of the Apparently Drowned.' I had somehow been expecting a heady brew of imperialist values, but what we see is a practical and sensible education in seamanship, such as the above, for even in my day it has not been normal for seafarers and fishermen to learn to swim, the prevailing philosophy apparently being that of the lighthouse keeper who said, 'If you're to drown, it's worse for the ones who can swim.'

However, the college was not free and it was intended for gentlemen. The regulations stipulated that:

– [....] Any valuable Gold Watches or Chains brought by Cadets will be taken from them and placed in security until the Cadets return home. Silver Watches may be used.

– [....] Cadets are not permitted to open accounts with Tradesmen. Parents and Guardians are requested not to allow their sons' outfitters to supply clothes or other articles without their authorisation.

They had to take care of their valuables. The 1946 play *The Winslow Boy* by Terence Rattigan was based on a notorious incident that took place at Osborne in 1908 while Max was there. George Archer-Shee was just thirteen when he was accused of stealing a five-shilling postal order from another cadet's locker and cashing it at the post office. There was an investigation at the college and the boy was expelled in shame. However, his parents did not let the matter go and after a well-publicized trial he was acquitted and even received an apology from the Admiralty.

One of Max's fellow cadets was 'Parnell, Hon. J.B. Born 17th May 92,' the same year as Max, and enrolled as a cadet in the same term. Together they went from Osborne to Dartmouth and from there on to their first ships. Max was a midshipman in 1909, then the *London Gazette* reports in 1912 from the Admiralty 'that Acting Sub-Lieutenant Maximilian Carden Despard has been promoted to the rank of Sub-Lieutenant.' He served on a number of ships leading up to the outbreak of war: the *Albemarle* (1909–10), the *London*, the *Minerva*, the *Indomitable*, the *Invincible*, the *Shannon*, the *Blenheim*, the *Indefatigable*, the *Pembroke*. His first report was not favourable, saying: 'A very slow boy[.] Seems to have outgrown his strength and inclined to be lazy.' From then on he is reported as 'promising' and goes from being 'zealous' to 'a most capable young officer,' 'intelligent' and 'an officer of great power of leadership, good influence, tactful, strong personality.'

As a sub-lieutenant Max served on the battle-cruiser HMS *Indefatigable* in August 1914 in the lead up to hostilities. He was present in the pursuit of the *Goebben* and *Breslau* under Admiral Sir Archibald 'Arky-Barky' Milne. This was a wild-goose chase round the Mediterranean which culminated in the German ships reaching Turkish waters after violating neutral Italian waters. It was altogether an unfortunate event. It also resulted in the court martial of Admiral Sir Ernest Troubridge, who had refused the order to pursue the vessels. However, on 18 September 1914 the *London Gazette* reports that Max has been promoted to Lieutenant. He was to be promoted to Lieutenant-Commander in 1922 and Commander (retired) in 1932.

Max, circa 1913.

Important to his future career were the references and letters of recommendation from his early ships. On 20 August 1912 the captain of HMS *Invincible* says he is a 'good and capable young officer whose services I am sorry to lose.' Two years later, on 23 September 1914, G.C. Dickens, Commander of HMS *Blenheim*, recalls him 'with zeal and ability and entirely to my satisfaction.' And on 5 March 1916 the captain of HMS *Penelope* says he is 'very much to my satisfaction. A clever and capable officer – considerably above the average ability. I am very sorry to lose him.'

When he was on the *Penelope* Europe was at war. Max sends a Christmas card with a picture of the ship and some generously accented French: *A Winter patrol our bête noire.*

The Broke.

The *Broke*

I shall all ways consider it the greatest of honour to have been Commander Evans' 1ˢᵗ Lieutenant, and 1ˢᵗ Lieutenant of H.M.S. "Broke"

Max was fortunate. It is impossible to write the story of Max without saying something about Teddy Evans, later Lord Mountevans. Edward Ratcliffe Garth Russell Evans was the son of a London barrister. By 1914 he was already famous as an Antarctic explorer. Evans first went south in 1902 on a relief expedition to fetch Captain Scott. Scott's ship, the *Discovery,* was trapped in ice and not until 1904 did Evans return on the *Terra Nova* to blast the *Discovery* out of the ice. Evans then served as second-in-command on Captain Scott's fateful journey of 1910–13 and he was captain of the *Terra Nova*. Evans writes cautiously about Scott, but Roland Huntford in *Shackleton* (1997) quotes the dog driver Cecil Meares as saying that 'Captain Scott would swear all day at [Teddy] Evans and the others.' Scott did not include Evans on the final lap of the journey to the South Pole. Scott admired Evans as a sailor more than as an explorer on land. The two men were not on the best of terms, perhaps because Scott considered Evans a rival. No wonder: Evans was decisive, impulsive and warm-hearted, whereas there was a reserve about Scott. Scott had not succeeded with ponies, dogs or motor sledges, and by now the men were pulling the sledges themselves, burning precious calories. Evans had been in charge of the hopeless sledges and he and his team were exhausted. Within 150 miles of the Pole and still 100 miles from base camp Evans was turned back with two other men. In the end they had to strap him onto the sledge as he was on the point of death from scurvy. They did not leave him behind as he had ordered; as he said, this was the only time in his naval career that his orders were disobeyed. In 1912 he returned to the Antarctic for a second time to bring Scott home.

Evans was short and wiry, exceedingly fit. He was a great swimmer and would dive into the water at odd times in his 'antiquated bathing suit.' Once in an emergency he left the dinner table to rescue the crew of a steamer. 'In a few minutes our lovely best monkey-jackets were saturated.' When Admiral Keyes left Ostend, Evans swam out in the wake of the departing flagship. He loved showing off – tearing packs of cards in two, doing handstands at formal dinners – and his 1963 biographer Reginald Pound tells us that in New Zealand he once lifted a lady by the belt of her dress and with his teeth carried her round the tennis-court, a variation on one of his party pieces. He had a tremendous and spontaneous gift with people. Once when making a speech during the war he noticed a sailor in the crowd and immediately drew him up on the platform to honour him and his kind.

I only wish I had met him. However, I did meet his Norwegian wife, by then Lady Mountevans. (She was rather overwhelmed at being elevated into the peerage. Once, in Harrods, she titled herself Lady Mountbatten. However, it is to her credit that she told the story herself.) I met her on the narrow part of the path to the beach in the small fishing village of Ula in Norway. I was a very small child and can only remember three large ladies in white bearing down on me with cries of enthusiasm. I was highly embarrassed, scowled, and did not rise to the occasion, too young to see that they may have been touched at seeing the youngest child of Max and Lilanna.

Teddy Evans's independence and daring were to write him into history and make him 'Evans of the *Broke*,' a household name at one time. The ship was named after Sir Phillip Broke, commander of the *Shannon* in the victory over the American vessel *Chesapeake* off Boston in 1813. This is how Evans in his 1946 autobiography *Adventurous Life* describes the *Broke*, the ship in which the Second Battle of Dover Strait was fought and the vessel which made the naval careers of both Evans and his lieutenant-commander, Max Despard:

> One of the things that surprised the Dover destroyer people visiting the *Broke* was that we carried ten Marines. Marines in a destroyer! My Captain pals had never heard of such a thing. The *Broke* was certainly a comfortable ship, beautiful in a sea-way, with splendid bridge accommodation, although, like the poor little *Flirt*, she had a habit of covering herself with cinders. She was originally built for the Chilean Navy and had spacious Captain's quarters and "rotten" quarters for everyone else! She had been "requisitioned" before delivery from the Chilean Government, under the 1914 Emergency War programme, when her name was changed from *Almirante Goni*. Her speed was 29 knots and her principal fuel, as stated, was coal.
>
> One remarkable feature about this ship was the disposition of her gun armament. We could fire four 4-inch guns right ahead.

The incident which was one of the few bright spots in the Allies' sea war occurred on the night of 20–21 April 1917. The *Broke* and the *Swift*, the two destroyers on the Dover patrol, suddenly became aware of several German ships: whether there were five, six or even

Max (left) with Teddy Evans on the Harebell, 1925.

seven is uncertain. The *Swift* lived up to her name and rapidly attacked and hit one ship. The enemy was not aware of the *Broke*. The *Broke*'s first lieutenant sent a torpedo that scored a direct hit on the next ship and sank it. That first lieutenant was my father, 'the beautiful Max Despard,' as Evans described him. Then Evans ordered full speed and let the *Broke* ram the next ship sideways. The ships were locked into each other. Then some of the German seamen, 'a number of frenzied Germans,' according to the Glasgow *Evening News*, boarded the *Broke*. For the first and surely the last time in a destroyer the signal was piped: *Repel Boarders*. By Max. And the boarders were repulsed. The fighting was hand-to-hand – with pistols, bayonets, sabres and cutlasses. Finally the remaining German ships slunk into the night. On board the *Broke* were twenty-two dead or dying and twenty-seven wounded. The ship had to be towed to Dover.

Cutlasses?

And did they put down sawdust on the decks?

This is how the Glasgow *Evening News* reported the story on 26 April, for once good news at a time when each day brought fresh reports of deaths on the Western Front. The headlines are bold: '**A THRILLING STORY – DOVER SEA FIGHT – A MIDSHIPMAN'S DUEL** A stirring account of the successful fight between destroyers of the Dover patrol and German destroyers on 20th inst. has been issued by the Press Bureau.' The boarding and the ramming are vividly described by the reporter. He must have pieced the story together through interviews. The newspaper account made much of the brave midshipman who met the frenzied Germans:

> The midshipman, amid the dead and wounded of his guns crews and half blinded by blood, met the rush single-handed with an automatic revolver. He was grappled by a German who attempted to wrest the weapon from him. Cutlasses and rifles with fixed bayonets being among the equipment of the foremost guns' crews in anticipation of just such events as were now taking place, the German was promptly bayoneted by Able Seaman Ingleson.

Evans writes about the battle, with his usual gusto, 'I must say I thoroughly enjoyed myself, although at one time I was very frightened.' He goes on:

> Despard was watching the torpedo he had fired speeding through the water, and quite suddenly he yelled out, "We've got her!" There was a bright flash and we knew that our torpedo had reached its mark. It had got a destroyer plumb amidships. My intention had been to ram this vessel, but it was not now necessary to do so. [....] In fine

weather we always kept three loaded rifles with bayonets fixed at each gun, and one at each torpedo-tube and after-searchlight. Cutlasses were provided all round the upper deck, besides which revolvers were supplied to petty officers, and there were many kept loaded on the bridge. The anti-aircraft pom-poms were also manned and, at the moment of ramming, when Lieutenant Despard piped, "Boarders on the forecastle", the weapons practically fell into the hands of the men who were waiting to use them. [….] Up on the bridge we had quite a merry time.

About the aftermath of the fight he wrote:

After seeing that everything possible had been done for our wounded, I went down to the mess-deck to tell my ship's company what had happened in the fight and generally to congratulate and cheer them, but to my astonishment, I found over 100 German prisoners being served with a fine fried-egg-and-bacon breakfast and waited on by our cheerful seamen and stokers as if they had been a visiting football team!

Of the humorous incidents, perhaps that which interested me most was in the heat of the fight, when our Mr. Smith, looking at the huddled mass of enemy sailors on the deck of *G.42,* seized two of the Webley Scott revolvers and, exclaiming "Here, Mr. Despard, now's your chance!" handed these to the First Lieutenant, and took two more pistols himself. I shall not forget seeing these two men, who blazed off altogether 60 rounds. I am shocked to say my coxswain and others even threw our cups of hot cocoa at the enemy!

This is strange reading. What were my feelings on reading this narrative, which in essence is horrific? My emotions have been conditioned by other accounts I have read of the First World War. I am an English teacher and a poet. Max's world was not my world. My experience of war has come from Wilfred Owen and Siegfried Sassoon. They made it their task to write about the pain of war, the shuffling columns of gassed men. I have fortunately no experience of violence and I have been educated to loathe war. Yet, although I cannot share Captain Evans's sense of humour, I find myself excited by the tale. I know the outcome and yet am carried away by its momentum. The 'frenzied Germans' take me back to Jim Hawkins defending the palisade from Long John Silver and his crew. The reason for my response must be the style; the brisk pace of the narrative belies the horrors of the encounter, presented almost as a boys' adventure. Though there were German submarines and though the terror of being torpedoed was ever present, this was written by combatants in what was, for many sailors, their first experience of combat – certainly of hand-to-hand fighting. The trench war dragged on with its merciless shelling, its mud and misery, day after day, month after month, but seamen in the First World War had fewer encounters. They were concerned with the business of war, its skills and techniques. They had not read Sassoon or Owen and would most likely not have approved of them. The *Evening News* journalist, Evans and my father wrote with pride, and they were careful not to shock our sensibilities. Moreover, the censor was vigilant, looking for any unpatriotic sentiment.

The battle was rendered in fiction in Taffrail's *Endless Story*. 'Taffrail' was the pseudonym of Captain Henry Taprell Dorling who wrote a series of popular books on ships and life at sea. He served on destroyers during the war and it is quite possible he was present on the *Broke*. As the book was published in 1931 he had no need to be wary of the censor. Certainly his account is vivid and gory:

Under heavy fire, a in a coruscation of gun-flashes and the sparkle and smoke of exploding shells, Evans put his helm over and drove straight for the enemy at 27 knots. There was hardly time to breathe, let alone to think coherently. The German, G.42, increased speed, smoke and showers of sparks pouring from her funnels as she strove to escape. But it was too late. With a grinding thud, and the screech of tearing steel, the *Broke*'s bow crashed into her opponent's port side abreast the after funnel.

It is impossible to describe the sensations of those on board both these ships as the collision occurred – the *Broke*'s grimly triumphant; the Germans filled with terror-stricken amazement and horror. It was a dreadful moment; but worse was yet to come.

Men were screaming and shouting for help as the *Broke*'s guns, at their maximum depression, pumped shell after shell at a few yards' range into the mass of men huddled on the deck of her stricken enemy...

But the *Broke* did not escape unpunished...She was blazing amidships...In the space of a few moments the *Broke* was converted into a smoking shambles, in places, her decks were literally running with blood.

When I was doing my A levels we were treated as real students and sent off to the public library to do research. On one of these trips and between the dreary shelves of the Sevenoaks Public Library I found a book that caught my interest. It was by Evans, whose name I knew. I looked for mention of my father and was gratified to see that he was described as 'beautiful.' However, I then came across a passage where they left German sailors lying in the sea, begging for mercy. I read the book hastily and furtively, troubled by this insight. I did not mention the book to my friend Gillian, my teacher or my sister Anita. Nor did I think of borrowing it to check the facts. The following is what I probably read and misread:

> Possibly phosphorescence was responsible for what we saw, but the swimming Germans appeared to have some calcium-light fitting in the life-saving waistcoats which they wore, and this we thought made a flicker of flame in the water to which we attributed the number of twinkling lights that could be seen in the sea all round us; these flickered and blinked like fairy lights on pantomime elves. The unfortunate Germans cried out "Save, save!" but the action was not yet finished, and although we eventually picked up a number of them, when my First Lieutenant asked me whether I would not stop then and lower boats I told him that I was out to finish the fight first, and that we were not there to attend on midnight bathers!

I was happy to see that my father had shown compassion. 'Midnight bathers' is a callous remark and must seem so both to combatants and non-combatants alike. It clearly troubled Evans's biographer Reginald Pound and it cannot be left hanging in the air. War at sea is cruel, emotions run high; there is little time for deliberation. Ethical distinctions may become blurred in the heat. However, there were rules for the taking of prisoners, drawn up in 1864 in the first of the Geneva Conventions inspired by Henri Dunant. Twelve European nations signed a treaty guaranteeing the protection of prisoners and civilians in wartime. The wording of the Geneva Convention as drawn up after the First World War was based on this first conference: 'Belligerents must treat members of the enemy force who are wounded, sick or shipwrecked as carefully as they would their own.'

In his own book Evans justifies his severity on the grounds of the Germans' deception. The *Broke* had heard cries of 'Save Save!'

and hastened to help a burning ship. When they approached they were fired at. This part is unclear to me: Max writes that 'someone fired a shot over us.' Does this mean the undisciplined action of one member of the German crew, or was it a planned deception? If the latter, it broke all the rules of seamanship and conduct in war. Evans clearly had these rules of conduct in mind when he taunted the Germans with the *Lusitania,* a highly emotive name. When the luxurious Cunard liner *Lusitania* was torpedoed by a German U-boat on 7 May 1915 off the Irish coast she sank in eighteen minutes. Over a thousand passengers died, including a hundred children and many Americans. This was one of the reasons why America entered the war. As to hospital ships, during the First World War many passenger ships were converted to hospital ships and were clearly marked as such. The Hague Convention X of 1907 had set down clear regulations governing these ships; they were to be inspected to ensure that they were not carrying weapons or armed forces. The Germans chose to define the Allied hospital ships as troop ships and many were sunk by their mines and torpedoes.

It was not in Evans's nature to let men drown. It is unclear when the 'visiting football team' was taken prisoner, but altogether the *Swift* and the *Broke* rescued 140 Germans, according to Pound. In 1921 Evans spectacularly rescued Chinese sailors from the shipwrecked *Hong Moh*, stripping down and swimming through the waves with a line with great danger to himself.

Max describes the fight to his parents in a letter, dated 28 April, that is less histrionic and more technical than the newspaper report:

> I am writing to give you as much of an account of our little scrap as is possible. Please don't communicate anything to the Press but you can show this to anyone else you like.

As you no doubt understand, I am nearly worried out of my life, writing letters to relatives of killed and wounded, writing reports, making out defect lists, showing curious spectators and big wigs round the Ship, and generally trying to keep my head, very hard with the amount of alcohol offered one [...]

We were very lucky in sighting enemy, but we take all the credit for being ready for the unexpected, and for having a concise plan of action, which everybody knew, so there was no necessity for orders. The only Order I received was "Go on No. 1" from the Captain, on sighting the enemy. Even although I may not get anything out of this, I shall all ways consider it the greatest of honour to have been Commander Evans' 1st Lieutenant, and 1st Lieutenant of H.M.S. "Broke", and no Officer was ever served better than myself by any Ship's company, notwithstanding the fact that we lost 35?% [?] of Ship's company in casualties in the first two minutes.[....]

As all the above has appeared in the papers, I do not think the Censor will touch this. If he does, he will probably return the whole thing to me. We were pretty badly knocked about, but it is all rather superficial. I expect to get leave on Monday, 13th, about for, I hope 14–21 days.

Max writes another letter home on 30 April:

Sorry you are so agitated, but there is no necessity as I am absolutely fit, and in fact have never felt better. I wrote you a long epistle on the 27th April, as soon as it was possible, as the Censor would have stopped it before and probably has now. You must excuse this scrawl, as I am writing it in bed at 10.30 a.m. Very lazy of me! [The letter as it exists is printed and copied.] [...] I am at present Acting Captain of the "Bus" as the "Owner" has got a temporary job for a month or so. I hope to get leave on the 14th May. We were quite badly knocked about.

[…]We picked up no one ourselves, as they fired on us after they surrendered, except one who came alongside in a boat at daylight by himself, and two who were found in the f'cle pretending to be dead. It was with the greatest difficulty I prevented the sailors from hanging them.

This was Max's first experience of death. Twenty-two men died in the action. Bayonets were used. They cannot all have died instantly as in cowboy films. Max must have seen some of the men and boys writhing, some screaming, weeping, calling for their mothers. He could not write of these things even if he had wanted to. *Boys' Own* was what the censor demanded and the British public wanted and needed. The action soon brought its rewards. The *London Gazette* reports the NAVAL DESPATCH dated 10 May 1917:

The KING (is) pleased to give orders for the appointment of the undermentioned Officers to be Companions of the **Distinguished Service Order**, in recognition of their services in command of H.M.S. "Swift" and H.M.S. "Broke" respectively on the night of the 20th to 21st April, 1917, when they successfully engaged a flotilla of five or six German destroyers, of which two were sunk:

Cdr. (now Capt.) Ambrose Maynard Peck, R.N.

Cdr. (now Capt.) Edward Ratcliffe Garth Russell Evans, C.B., R.N.

The KING has further been graciously **pleased** to give orders for the award of the **Distinguished Service Cross** to the undermentioned Officers for their services during this action:

[among which] Lieut. Maximilian Carden Despard, R.N. First

and Gunnery Lieut of H.M.S. "Broke". He controlled gun fire and gave the orders which resulted in an enemy destroyer being torpedoed.

Three officers, one gunner, one surgeon and one midshipman from the *Broke* were awarded the DSC. The officers were Commander E.R.G.R. Evans, Lieutenant G.B. Hickman and Lieutenant M.C. Despard. The DSC – a third level decoration – was awarded 'in recognition of exemplary gallantry during active operations against the enemy at sea.' Since 1993 it has been extended to all ranks of the armed forces.

ZEEBRUGGE.   (INTREPID. - IPHIGENIMA. - THITIS)   PHOTO G.Pottier

Some of the devastation seen in Belgium after the war.

Ostend

The immediate postwar years were good for Max. He is still under the command – and, I imagine, the spell – of Teddy Evans. There was not only the *Broke* operation; altogether the Dover patrol had been a great success. Evans was proud that they had not lost one soldier escorting troops across to the Continent during the war. Now immediately after the war Evans had a new appointment:

> Senior Naval Officer at Ostend, where I was to take charge and clear up outstanding naval commitments on the Belgian coast. [....] Anyway, I got down to it, and acquired a lot of lively officers including my beloved and handsome Despard, who like the others, understood my language, and, what is more, understood that when there was a job to do it had got to be done at once. They also understood that when there was a game to play we must all play our hardest.

Mostly salvage is the hard and tedious work that follows a war, tidying up the mess on the coast and clearing sunken wrecks from the sea, yet Evans describes the work with his customary gusto: 'Salvage is a disappointing business at the best of times: it is rather like trout-fishing in a way, that men spend days and months, and sometimes years, in salving ships and attempting to recover treasures that the sea has swallowed up.'

Evans was amazed to see the docks at Bruges where the Germans had rested in comfort between their submarine raids. He was gratified to find a destroyer that had been torpedoed in the bows: 'From her log-book she appeared to have been one of the six that the Swift and Broke had engaged on the night of 20th–21st April 1917.'

Evans was placed in command of the Auxiliary Command, more specifically the Fishery, Minesweeping and Patrol Services. The Svalbard Treaty was first signed in 1920, giving sovereignty over Spitsbergen to Norway. The Russians did not always agree to its terms, but recently, in 2010, Russia and Norway signed 'The Treaty on Maritime Delimitation and Cooperation in the Barents Sea and Arctic Ocean' after decades of negotiation, so it is interesting to read Evans's description of the geopolitical tangles in these cold waters:

The sloops *Harebell* and *Godetia* were patrolling off the Murmansk coast, well up in the Arctic, when I took over control.

It was a beastly business, this winter patrolling, but however bad it may have been for our fellows in the *Harebell* and *Godetia* it must have been worse, far worse, for the trawlers they were protecting against the unwarranted interference by the *Yaroslavna*, and other armed ships of the Soviet republic. It was an ice-bound business, anyhow, and its one redeeming feature was the unusual experience gained and the kindness of the Norwegians in the ports which our ships used as bases.

It may be of interest to state here why the trawlers from Hull, Grimsby and Scarborough fished in these far Northern waters. The stock of plaice is distributed over three chief grounds, the North sea, Iceland and, for want of better name, the Barents Sea, which really means the waters to the northward of Arctic Scandinavia and the Murman coast. [....]

The British standpoint has always been that outside the three-mile limit is the High Seas, wherein every nation has a right to fish at all times of the year. Norway claimed a four-mile limit, whilst Russia insisted upon a twelve-mile limit, to which we have never agreed.

Cases of arresting our ships led to deputations of trawler owners visiting the Admiralty and protesting, and when, after what we considered to be unwarranted interference and arrest, a British trawler was wrecked through the negligence of its Soviet captors, the situation had to be dealt with firmly. In consequence a Northern Fishery Protection Service was inaugurated, hence the *Harebell*'s and *Godetia*'s Arctic Patrol.

But just about this time Ireland was being a little unkind, and at the same time the Captain of the *Doon* reported from the Irish Sea Patrol that about a thousand rounds of ammunition had been fired by a rough-and-tumble crowd at his trawler gunboat. He had replied by firing a 12-pounder, which knocked the side off an Irish pub. [According to Pound the *Doon*'s captain said the shots went on either side of the pub.] Besides this, the Norwegian fishery cruisers, the old-fashioned coast defence ships *Tordenskjold* and *Heimdal*, had also made some arrests. Mines were still popping up into drifters' nets and being caught up in trawls, fishermen were clamouring for something substantial in the way of compensation for their war services, the Auxiliary Patrol itself was bleating because they had had no promotions, and generally speaking, I found that I had a rocky time ahead.

There were compensations and relief from the plaice war. Evans arranged a fishing expedition to Iceland: 'Despard and Pope, another lieutenant from the *Harebell*, and my surgeon friend Arthur Cheattle, who had come with me as a guest, comprised my party.' Evans writes

Max fishing for salmon in Iceland, 1920.

lyrically of the glittering snow-covered mountains, 'the well-man-nered sturdy little mountain-bred ponies' and the hospitable people, descendants of the Vikings:

> All the dirty stoke-hole work or the monotonous handling of sail will be forgotten when one looks on the Icelandic mountains. When I saw them first I felt homesick for Norway, to which this unvisited land is akin. I longed to be running on ski over snow slopes, or to hear the musical gurgle of the mountain torrents, and to see the summer waterfalls from the melting glaciers.

No wonder he longed for Norway, 'the northern fairyland' as he called it. In 1916 he had married Elsa Andvord, his 'Viking bride.' The love affair with Norway lasted until the end of his life. In his final illness he was at the Andvords' mountain cabin at Gålå in Norway and died there in 1957.

Max's job had more compensations than fishing trips. He did not spend his whole time in icy waters; in Ostend his work was mainly sedentary and administrative, which did not seem to worry him unduly. He seems very pleased with himself in the letter he writes to his father in May 1920:

My dear Pa,

I seem to have established myself on an office chair here and have quite a lot to do at present we are just turning over HQ from Dunkerque to here & I am doing my best to organise our new base and instil a little discipline into a somewhat ungainly gang of pirates we have about 600 ratings of various sorts under us including Salvage Ratings (biggest pirates) R.M. Engineers, Naval M.T H.Q.Staff and one or two other odds and ends. I have various titles including Chief Staff Officer. Asst. to S.N.O, 1st Lieut and one or two others. I draw the enormous stipend of 33/- a day about £700 a year but most of it goes to live as far as I can see, everything is about four times more expensive than in England. Six of us have a house the rent of which comes to 600 francs a month[…] I don't think I shall save much with cocktails at 2.50 beer 2.0 & a small box of chocolates 5.0 fr a cup of tea 1.50 and so on. I think it promises to be quite interesting as things go on and some of the wreckage gets cleared up and the base opens up. At present organising work is a nuisance but it will soon settle down and I don't think I shall go greyhaired. I have a Rolls-Royce car at my disposal which I trot about in. In time I shall no doubt develop a fur collar to my coat and a cigar and the staff air.

Not only does Max have splendid titles and a Rolls-Royce to trot about in, he is also setting himself up with a manservant and clearly has plans of his own. He is twenty-eight years old. On 11 August he writes to his father from Naval Headquarters, Ostend:

> I will look around for a man servant of my own. [?] is too old but the wages they are asking is anything from £80–£120 so I am afraid there will be nothing doing.
>
> What I want to do is some courses in Gunnery Torpedo etc and refresh my memory as after all it is 8 years since I have done any and things have changed a bit.
>
> I will try to get home for a day or two as I want to see Mrs Moore.

His career prospects are good and he is collecting medals. In 1919 Portugal awarded him the order Chevalier of the Military Order of the Tower and Sword. In 1920 he became Chevalier of the Order of the Crown of Belgium. Later that year he writes to his father, 'I see I get about seven years to my War medal:'

1. Mediterranean 1914
2. North Sea 1915
3. North Sea 1916
4. Narrow Seas 1917
5. Belgian Coast 1917
6. Swift and Broke
7. Home Seas 1918

I have seen these medals on photographs of Max in uniform – but for decades their whereabouts has been unknown.

And who is Mrs Moore?

The Danube

When Shakespeare in *Julius Caesar* used the term 'let slip the dogs of war' he predicted the horrors that would ensue from one reckless act. The shot in Sarajevo in 1914 has been pinpointed as the start of the Great War. The assassin Gavrilo Princip had been armed and paid by the Serbian organization the 'Black Hand' to kill the Archduke Ferdinand and his wife. (Princip is still honoured by Serbs, while Croats and Bosniak children learn that he was a terrorist assassin.) During the war Serbs and Montenegrins fought with the Allies and established close ties to Britain and France, while Bulgaria chose the other side. Romania fought with the Allies – at the 'last minute' some said, though it was in fact after 1916. There were complicated reasons for choice of side in each case. Among many fervent passions, the Bulgarians hated the Turks, while Romanians hated Hungarians and feared the Russians. After the Great War a new order was established on the Continent. The Austro-Hungarian Empire – the vestiges of the Holy Roman Empire – had been defeated and dissolved. The Ottoman Empire was dissolved by the war, to be replaced by the new Turkish Republic. The Empire of the Tsar was broken but a new power was establishing itself in its stead: the Union of Soviet Socialist Republics, or USSR. Two new states had been created at the conference tables: Czechoslovakia and Yugoslavia. In Yugoslavia the Serbs had the upper hand. They had suffered greatly in the war and they had a powerful army. Both

Fisherman on the Danube, circa 1920.

Croats and Slovenes paid lip-service to the new state, and it seems that the imposed unity was only skin-deep.

Railways are national; waterways are international. One of the most important waterways of Europe is the Danube. At the end of the war a vacuum was left in the control of the river and Admiral Troubridge was appointed to fill the gap and re-establish the Commission internationale du Danube, or CID. At the same time the Danube Navigation Company, largely British-owned, secured the river assets left by the Central Powers. The traffic on the river was to a large extent British, most importantly Shell taking oil from Romania.

The Danube near Orsova, circa 1920.

And here is Max, an active sailor. As a young lieutenant he was given a position of immense trust, virtually left in charge of navigation on the Danube. Troubridge believed in Max. It must also have been to Max's advantage that he had experience of salvage from Ostend. The Danube was cluttered with wreckage after the war. Max was seconded from the Admiralty, appointed to the Orsova section of the CID. Orsova is the port closest to the strategically important Iron Gates, the point where the river narrows and the currents are fierce. Max's task was to bring about the re-establishment of the commission in a new guise. This was a curious posting for a naval officer, and the Admiralty took exception to paying Max as an active officer and proposed to the Foreign Office that his costs and those of the three seamen – his staff – should be covered by the Foreign Office. The correspondence went to and fro for a while, uncomfortable for Max and not the only time in his life when he would be caught between two administrative bodies.

I tried to read Claudio Magris' celebrated 1986 work *Danubio* to learn more about the Danube, but his world was not that of Max. My father had to contend with sandbanks, wrecks, Greek pilots, Romanian customs officers and all the officialdom of a new, badly welded state. The Danube has its source in Germany, and runs through Austria, Czechoslovakia, Hungary and Yugoslavia (as were), forming the border between Bulgaria and Romania and ending in the Black Sea. It flows through the capital cities Vienna, Budapest and Belgrade. The Commission européenne du Danube was originally established in 1856 after the Crimean War, mainly with authority over the mouths of the river, not only to police the river, but to secure dykes and canals in the marshy delta. It was an international body with sovereignty over the river; indeed, it was compared to the League of Nations. Though not always efficient, its power was such that it was described as 'glimmering' in the 'twilight of statehood.' In 1920–1 after the Treaty of Versailles the CID was organized to secure the Danube as an international waterway and to control the traffic on the upper reaches of the river. As Bucharest, the capital of Romania, does not lie on the river, Orsova, a port midway between Belgrade and Bucharest, became a vital point.

The aim was to ensure peace on this, Europe's second largest river. Peace was perhaps too much to hope for as there were too many vying interests. In addition to ethnic conflicts there were differences of religion that were not always identical with ethnic or linguistic differences. Slavs hated Muslims, though many Muslims were linguistically Slavs. Muslims hated Christians, and Christians hated each other: Greek Orthodox pitted against Roman Catholics.

Yet 'hate' is too sweeping a term and not fair; in many places people coexisted quite peacefully. What is certain is that the riparian states Bulgaria and Romania resented being administered by an Anglo-French body. Then there was the greed for the vast natural resources, such as the oil from Romania, oil that was to play a central part in a later chapter in Max's life.

Max served as Representative of the Iron Gates Section from May 1920 to October 1921 and he faced formidable obstacles in this, his first proper job on shore – and very different from his experience in Ostend. On 1 July 1920 he sends his father a copy of a letter to 'a bloke in charge of my dept. at the Admiralty.' The spelling is not his but that of his American-German typist interpreter. The following is a sketch of his proceedings and also a few opinions:

> I took over from Fletcher on 24 May about. It was obvious that there was someting radically wrong with the whole administration of the Section. The local officials were all up in arms against the Commission, they did not trust the Commission, they considered that the policy was neither unbiessed or impartial.
>
> My predecessor held strong anti Roumanian opinions, the result of actions of the Roumanians earlier in the year which had forced him into a position from which he could not withdraw [...] My position was decidedly unpleasant. Fletcher had forcibly ejected a secret police agent from a dinner party just before he left, under circumstances which gave him the greatest provocation, thus accenting the anti Commission feeling among the Roumanian population, and also, due to very active anti British propaganda, anti British feeling. [...]

Max is a young man, full of energy, and is determined to get down to work: 'I decided to go into everything thoroughly and to reorganize

Danube pilots.

the whole outfit making it as international as possible and endeavour to remove all causes of irritation.' He is forthright and thorough in his dealings with the employees:

I saw all the staff and pilots and gave them strict orders with re-gard to their conduct and dealing with officials and that I would not countenance any word or action on their part detrimental to the authority of the state that the resided in. I had a look around the section, at signal arrangements and buoyage. I went into administra-tion and the financial side, drew up schemes for the revision of pay & conditions of service, pensions and the conditions for pensions.

He then writes about his many meetings with senior Romanian officials, including one about settling the affair of Fletcher, who had hit his dinner guest. 'I told the minister that there were at present only two courses open to the Roumanians: 1./ was to accept me provisionally as I was here and intended staying, and to work with me. 2./ was to continue to obstruct me.' He has little faith in the Romanians:

> The Roumanians cannot in any way be considered as fully civilised, they Roumanians realise they are not as advanced as western powers, and if they can do a thing behind your back, they will, and merely think it a good stroke of work and not that it is dishonest... Their actions should therefore not be construed in the same way as one would of those of a western power with a civilitation of countless years, but rather as the actions of a man who was brought up as a child by a wholehearted scoundrel.

He adds:

> Really the Turk at his worst was never as bad as the Roumanian, you can have no idea of the complete corruption of their whole administration. It is rotten through and through. There is only one power and that is the power to pay. They are in for a bad time but they wont see it they have swollen head badly and unless the administration is taken over by France and Brittain it surely will be quietly by Germany who will gradually work through Transalvania to get the power into their hands.

And yet Max adds in pencil to his father, 'I think this is quite the most amusing and interesting job I have had for some time. ... I am in complete control of the really most critical part of the river...the Iron Gates.' On 3 August he writes:

Things out here have settled down a good deal and people generally seem to be beginning to realise that one is trying to help them. I am now a representative of the International Commission, how long I shall be out here I cant tell as long as the Commission requires me I am afraid, it is really a very dull place when one has nothing to do. The whole of the Commission headed by Admiral Troubridge arrives here the day after tomorrow [...] The first time I have seen them since I have been out here.

This is important, as Max feels his status is unclear. 'I rather expect to be relieved by a civilian in October as it is hardly right I suppose to have a soldier or sailor acting in a foreign country in time of peace.' The meeting must have gone well, as on 12 August he adds to his idiosyncratically spelt letter:

The Commission have been and gone. The Admiral was in good spirits and they all seemed very complimentary so I seem to be in their good books as far as I can gather I will be here at least till the end of the year if not longer. They have agreed to everything I have done and greatly extended my power and included Turnu-Severin in my section, they have given me authority to deal direct with Belgrade and Bukarest in fact they seemed quite pleased to do anything I wanted.

My father was only twenty-eight, and took charge. The Balkan intrigues must have seemed bizarre and outlandish. Maybe the only way a young British officer could keep up his spirits among Romanians, Hungarians, Serbs, Montenegrins, Herzegovinians, Croats and Bosniaks, with all their various ethnic and religious ramifications, was to see the comic side of things, although it cannot have been amusing to represent an organization that was superimposed and un-wanted by many. There was also much hard work. One of the many things he had to deal with was to coordinate the various authorities that supervised the state of the river and to deal with any complaints that occurred. He saved one document and sent it to his father to show what he had to contend with. It concerns a Serb pilot, Anton Boschitz, sent to measure the depths of water at Golubach. When he landed he was ill-treated by the Romanian functionary. In the pilot's own words:

I went again to the bridge, where I had to wait the custom-house officer. Finally he came (I never saw him before) and demanded my passport. I gave him that one, I got from the Representative of the C.I.D. Orsova.

"You came with this passport?" he asked in Roumanian. Then he asked me, of which nationality I was. "Nyamc" I answered; at this moment I got a box on the left cheek.

"Ungur", he cried and cursed the Hungarian-English-and French nations. At once, the officer stroke me with his fist several times on the head and pushed me back into the room. There he continued to box me and asked again:

"Are you still Hungarian?"

The other above mentioned man knocked me with his fist between the eyes, that my blood run from the nose and mouth. As I was later told, he was the adjunct of the Roumanian Captain of Port, named Jonescu….The officer called me into the building and revised my pockets, where he found several insignificant papers, among the others also a printed-matter with the stamp of the Rep-resentative. Then he confiscated all my papers and legitimations, and commanded the soldier to lock me up again.

[....] the expressions prove quite evident, that the insult could happen to any one of the employees of the C.I.D.

This bizarre example of bad treatment is ominous when seen in the light of underlying conflicts in the region. It is a chilling reminder of the old rivalry between Romania and Hungary. After the First World War, Romania was given large territories that had been part of Hungary, and the Romanians gloated over their new gains. In Transylvania the majority of the population was Romanian. The minority was Hungarian but had the political and economic power. The last words of the pilot significantly reveal the delicate nature of the Danube commission in this troubled region: 'He will all exert still he is here, to make him difficulties and unpleasantness, because England and France have nothing to do with the Danube.'

These were the issues Max had to deal with. On 21 October 1920 he sent the document to his father:

It requires the temper of an angel dealing with some of the petty officials, the Commission seems to have no control over them. This fellow the Chief Customs Officer at Moldova knocked this pilot about with the assistance of the Deputy Captain of Port. The incident occurred at 7.pm in the evening and was telephoned down to me by one of my agents. I had to actually motor 100 kilometers to lug this fellow out of jail myself were he had been put on some trumped up charge. I then came down on the Customs Officer and his accessory like a ton of bricks two days afterwards with the head of his department. They are now both in jail. They are savages and tire me....I had a great day on Sunday spent all day out in the hills after pig and deer...However I am tired of this spot, one gets little peace and constant worries, one wearies of trying to help people who wont help themselves. People seem to think I am anything from a Cook's tourist bureau to a League of Nations Legation.

Although his job is wearying, it seems Max had the humour and the lack of respect for red tape that made him able to cope with situations such as these. He acquired knowledge of the river and the many peoples of the riparian states that was to stand him in good stead two decades later. He acquitted himself well in Orsova and received glowing reports in two languages, both for his technical work and for his personal qualities The British delegates to the Danube commission praise his charts of the Rapids Section of the river, they commend his report and inform 'the Lords Commissioners of the Admiralty that it was unanimously decided to express to Lieutenant M.C. Despard, D.S.C., R.N., the warm thanks of the Commission for the manner in which he had accomplished his functions as Representative at the Iron Gates Section during the period May 1920 to October 1921.' They then thank 'his Britannic Majesty's Government for so courteously allowing this Officer's invaluable services to remain at the disposition of the Commission throughout that time.' The French representative of the commission writes from Budapest in December 1921 to 'Monsieur le Lieutenant de Vaisseau, M.C. Despard, R.N., Londres' that they regret his departure and wish him all the best for 'la poursuite brillante de votre future carriere.'

Max has proved himself decisive and capable of hard work. He is also enjoying himself, hobnobbing with minor royalty such as 'the Crown Prince of Roumania whose only remark to me at one of the functions was "bloody awful show this isn't it wish we could get a drink". Seems quite a nice fellow.'

Leonora Brabazon Moore at the time of her marriage in 1921.

Nora

Max was not alone in Orsova.

Mrs Moore was the widow of the late Colonel Wardrup Moore, an energetic man in business and in pleasure. He and his companion Rosa were in San Francisco at the time of the 1906 earthquake; they were on their way to New Zealand, to fish. The Moores had a daughter: Leonora Brabazon Moore, or Nora.

The Moore fortunes came from coal. The family owned the Bent Colliery in the Lanarkshire field. They also had interests in the more profitable Hamilton Palace Colliery. New technology meant mines with deeper seams could now be exploited, and Hamilton Palace opened in 1884, the Bent Colliery Company having obtained a lease of mineral rights on the Duke of Hamilton's estates at Bothwell-haugh, between Hamilton and Motherwell in North Lanarkshire. At first the pit employed fourteen workers underground and six surface workers, but by the beginning of the twentieth century there was an output of almost 2,000 tons per day and 1,400 employees. Many Lithuanians worked in the Scottish mines, but many moved on to America. The village of Bothwellhaugh became known as the 'pailis' and included two churches, two schools, a Miners' Welfare Association, a cooperative store, houses and allotment gardens – but no pubs and no sale of alcohol. The mine brought vast incomes to the Hamiltons and to the Bent Colliery Company alike. Hamilton Palace was the largest non-royal residence in the Western world, visited by Queen Victoria and much admired. It was built in 1695 and pulled down in 1921 – undermined by its mine.

Nora was small and vivacious, rich and attractive. She and Max had known each other for years, as Nora was the best friend of Max's sister Ierne. However, it appears from Max's letters to his father that Nora's mother kept making difficulties and postponing the wedding. In 1919 Nora writes in her large handwriting to her future father-in-law:

> You know thanks to you all being so sweet to me I don't feel a bit like a stranger entering the family. Max and I have both received letters from Mother saying she gives her consent.
>
> This is quite a difficult letter to write you know so you must forgive it's somewhat rambling utterances! But I just want to say I'll try my very best to make the best sort of wife to Max and thank you so very much for giving him to me – this sounds awfully badly expressed I'm afraid but you will know what I mean.

Nora and Max had planned the wedding to suit his leave, but Nora's mother put a spoke in the wheel as she apparently had plans to go to Switzerland. Another possible reason is that she never thought Max quite good enough. This is Max writing and telegraphing to his father from Orsova on 1 December 1920:

> I am really furious with Mrs M she is a silly woman why the devil cant she write and tell me what she means instead of writing and saying she is frightened of spoiling Nora. Good God it is the one time in Nora's life which I think a mother can afford to spoil her only daughter a little […] I honestly think Mrs M Jack and Co are being exceedingly selfish.

Jack was Nora's brother; he was not an easy character and he was to cause difficulties for the family later. There are letters from my mother making clear that she has been left to cope with her husband's former in-laws. Aunt Rosa is one of the mythical figures I used to hear about. Herbert insists that when she came to stay at Bartley she arrived with a very heavy suitcase and left with one that was much lighter, clinking loudly as it was carried downstairs.

The plans for the wedding drag on, but finally they had a grand wedding in Scotland on 12 January 1921. What a good-looking couple they must have made: she so tiny, he so tall and splendid in his uniform. The local newspaper gave a full report of the DESPARD-MOORE WEDDING and the BRILLIANT CEREMONY IN HAMILTON EPISCOPAL CHURCH:

The church was beautifully decorated with masses of lillies [*sic*], pink and white flowers, palms etc. [...] The bride, who was given away by her brother Mr. J.W. Moore, looked charming in a draped gown of ivory satin beauté, with a long golden girdle and full train of gold brocade. Her bouquet was of lillies of the valley, the gift of the bridegroom [...] Tall and of fine carriage, the bridegroom, who was in full naval uniform and wore his medals and insignia of his several Orders, was attended by Lieutenant H.S. Simpson, D.S.C and bar, Royal Navy. [...] The happy couple left for Paris, where they will spend the earlier part of their honeymoon, afterwards proceeding to Roumania, where Lieutenant Despard holds his present appointment on the Danube.

The paper devoted an entire column to the gifts, among which there was much jewellery and silver, including two sets of silver bonbon dishes, 'doyleys' and a tablecloth. From Miss Despard to the bridegroom there was a shooting-stick, and from the bride's brother a picnic basket.

Before the wedding 'a deputation of the headquarters, Lanarkshire Constabulary, waited on Lieutenant M.C. Despard' to present him with 'a Sheraton cabinet fitted with an eight-day clock, cut glass decanters and smoker's outfit.' Constable Rankin in a most appropriate speech paid his respects to Max not only as the son of the chief constable but also as a fine young officer in the Royal Navy 'who had helped to keep them in their jobs at home during the war.' Max in turn, in thanking the headquarters staff for their magnificent present and for all the kind things they had said, remarked, 'I have been nearly all over the world and I can honestly say I have never seen a better type or a finer class of men than those serving in the Lanarkshire Constabulary.'

They left for Paris, the young bride in a beaver fur coat and hat to match. They spent much time in Switzerland, though Nora also visited Max in Orsova. He writes to his father of Nora picking primroses and skiing in the Serbian Alps. 'We have had a great time here Nora being as happy as a lark and in real great form, being burnt as brown as a berry and sparkling more than ever, she is locally known as "Sunshine."' Max observes that Evans could make himself unpopular through his constant publicity. 'I see Evans is in the limelight again – he has the luck of the old man – but I am afraid the continual apparance of his picture in the papers does him no good in the service with those who dont know him.'

Otherwise these letters are full of happiness. I have read one of their letters to Max's father. I say 'their' as they both write it, crisscrossing each other and commenting on each other's remarks. It is a letter full of banter and fun. She tells her father-in-law that they are busy decorating their house and that Max is an excellent upholsterer. They beg Herbert John to send out 'the Rabbit,' i.e. Ierne. 'I do **insist** on the Rabbit coming out. I feel sure Max will "cover" her with chintz and embraces.' Whereupon Max says in a typically brotherly way that this would need a fair amount of material. Max urges his father to send Ierne out with Miss Davis as companion:

> It is really an A1 opportunity for her and she will be able to travel with Miss Davis who will make all the arrangements and who is really an experienced and capable traveller. I am sending the Rabbit a cheque which will pay for her expenses in London and Paris and I will square up with Miss Davis for her travelling expenses.

In March 1921 'the Rabbit' writes to her father from Orsova:

> My Darling Pa,
> You would love it out here – it's such gorgeous country – and so wild – up in the hills it is perfectly lovely – Nora is very busy just now planning Max's birthday party for him. – judging from the amount of food she proposes giving him I rather think our little Max will bust. […] You cant get cigarettes out here – I would like 300 – I dont think I shall be home until the end of May or sometime in June – as Max wants us to take Nora back with us. Tons of love and a huge hug – and write to your poor Rabbit.

Max is getting used to being rich, living the good life on Nora's money. I would have liked a different father at this point: one who lived and thought rather like me and my friends. Max is no left-winger. In 1920 he wrote that he believed in 'the sanity of your working people.' His opinion is that 'the only Bolshies among British Labour are Irish, foreigners and youths. No sane labour man wishes to label himself "fool." Bolshevism is the cancer it must be cut out at the roots.' He goes on:

On the back of this circa 1922 photograph Nora has written "Mac looking specless [sic]! at Orsova". This is one of Nora's jokes.

It is good news Tommy being fixed up again with a job, specially a manager, has he said anything about it to you? I should say it was a good time to buy rubber as I see all rubber shares are showing a slow but distinct upward trend. Nora and I have been completely flummoxed by having to pay super tax on our last years income out of this years income we had to find £1200 to pay supertax out of an income of £200 which deducting income tax left us with a minus income. Happy days – We have had to borrow from the bank to do it. So far we have managed without realising capital and if the Bent pays 7½%–10% in May we may get square as we have no super tax to pay on this years income. Personally I should like to put £1000 in rubber and for a gamble I think Anglo-Persian oil to hold for five years. […] Nora gets home on the 19th if she can withstand the temptation of going to Paris to buy some clothes.

I hope Geoffrey is fitter.

Nora and I want to go to our first Derby this year. Will you come with us?

He asks about his younger brother Geoffrey's health. Geoffrey died on 17 March 1921. I have had to look it up twice as it was never mentioned among all the banter and financial concerns. Perhaps that was why they tried to get Herbert John to visit them. On 19 April Max writes to his father about the Scottish collieries. He is mainly concerned about Nora's dividends, but is sympathetic to his father, aware that a strike was a demanding time for a chief constable. Indeed Herbert John, a humane man, must often have seen the distress of the miners and their families in the many fatal accidents in the collieries. And now there was a strike which also involved the police force. The Scottish Mining Museum at Hamilton shows a photograph of the soup kitchen staff during the 1921 strike at the Bent

Colliery, an indication of the people's need. Max adds an important piece of news at the end of his letter:

You must be having a rotten time with this strike. I am so sorry for you as it must be most anxious work and worrying especially if it goes on much longer.

I expect Noras dividends from the Bent Co. will dwindle away to nothing this year as they have the expenses of the last strike to meet as well. If the Bent is flooded I doubt if it will be reopened. If the Palace is flooded I expect it will be quite six months before it is productive again. However the strike was bound to come. I only hope the Government and owners dont give way over the main points, although I think there is plenty of room for discussion on only the wage question.

Our interests are in the Bent and the Palace. The Bent was almost worked out anyhow and would have closed down in a year or two. The Palace is the best mining concern in Scotland and it will be a fearful shame if it is badly flooded as it will put, at least with the Bent 5000–6000 men out of work for six months.

About ourselves we are very fit. I expect Miss Davis will have given you all the news. We are very excited about Nora going to have a baby. October I expect.

In May Max writes to his father:

I shall be glad when Nora & Co. are safely at home. As I feel we are all sitting on a volcano in this part of the world, not a quiescent one by any means; but one which might erupt at any moment.[...]

The Commission offered me a permanent job as Commissioner for this port living at Orsova with 50,000 francs a year & a car. I am afraid though very flattering I didn't [?] it. So I remain here lent by the British Government till the permanent control is established.

I go up to Vienna with Nora & Co. Leaving her about the 13th spending about 4 days each in Belgrade, Budapest & Vienna and probably also in Paris.

I am really full up with work but so much office as in the role of diplomatic negotiator between the Commission & the Serbs & Rumanians. They seem to think I know them better than anyone else or am a more accomplished liar or whatever a diplomat should be. However, I am not going grey over it, & hope to be home in England for a month from the middle of October. Nora has taken a house in Gloucestershire "Holdfast Manor", "Upton on Severn", she wishes to be near a Doctor friend, a Dr. Thurstone. The Bent paid quite a respectable dividend so as long as we are careful we shall be O.K. in the future.

Nora adds to the letter:

Ierne no doubt gives you all the tit bits. (This bit is not to be censored by Mac!) By this modest letter of my little Husband's you will gather **how** pleased the People who Count in the Commission, are with Himself and his work, & from all the truly splendid things they said to me when we had some of them here last week you would with me swell yet larger with pride on this little son's account! It is quite extraordinary they think for so young a man to have such tact, clear views etc. with these rather slippery & difficult customers! [...]

It is just **awful** having to leave Mac here but let's hope in one way for him it won't be long –

Love to both from Nora

Nora's pride in Max is girlish, but it is based on the reports of his competence. Yet he feels this is not the right occupation for him; he does not enjoy being a diplomat rather than an active officer, and he does not enjoy being squeezed between the two sets of superiors. On 11 July he writes: 'I have chucked this job as the Admiralty wont go on paying me and I wont be paid by the C.I.D. – it means going on half pay. The Navy is my service so I am going back to it.' (Max hopes for a Motor Torpedo Boat as his next vessel.)

This relatively short period that Max spent in Romania was not the most important part of his career, but it is the period in which we as readers get to know him best. He is open and candid in the letters to his father, using him as a sounding-board for his worries or success in his work, his political views, his financial and family affairs. When Max returns to the Danube two decades later he will have no one to whom he can impart his written confidence. His father will not be there to receive his letters, and Max will also be constrained by diplomatic discretion.

In *Esprit de Corps* many years later, in 1957, Lawrence Durrell makes fun of the British Legation in Belgrade. He describes the invidious position of a naval attaché far from the sea: 'But who knows what obscure promptings may stir the heart of a naval attaché condemned to isolation in Belgrade, hundreds of dusty miles from the sound of the sea? And then, imagine being designated to a country with almost no recognizable fleet.'

Max does not attribute his frustrations to a longing for the ocean. He is deeply concerned about the state of Romania. In retrospect it seems as if its effete and corrupt government is already paving the way for Nicolae Ceausescu. When I pass the Romanian beggars in our local high street I think how prophetic Max was. 17 August 1921 he types out, or gets typed out, a letter summing up his thoughts on

Max, Nora and infant Terence, probably in Gloucestershire, 1921.

the post he is leaving. His troubles were not only due to the local population. His attitude to the Foreign Office is less than respectful. This will in time damage him. It is not clear to whom the letter was addressed, but he sends a copy to his father:

Having travelled about these balkanised countries a bit and having met and talked to many interesting men, business, political, soldiers and others perhaps my opinion may interest you.

Naturally not a word I write will be believed by the F.o. as they have their own people who keep them posted. Which leads me to a grouse which I may as well get off my chest.

It is a most extraordinary thing abroad the jealousy of Legation officials for soldiers or sailors, they seem to fear that we will take the bread and butter out of their mouths. Except for the Military Attache at Bucharest, Col. Duncan, of whom I see a lot, my existance is entirely ignored by the Legations in both Belgrade and Bucharest. Another point, one feels rather strongly is that the Legation of officials reside in the capital of the country and very seldom leave it, have thus really no first hand idea of conditions outside their capital, they also only come in contact with the best educated class and in consequence are inclined to judge the people and the country from them.

It makes me boil to see the whole of our Foreign Affairs subservient to the clang of the "Almighty Dollar" in these countries. It is hateful to hear sneering remarks like "oh the English they care for nothing but money now". I should have thought that it was an axiom that if you once establish the prestige of your country, for straight and square dealings, commerce will look after itself. It is no use lowering yourself to the level of the country you live in. Our policy in Roumania has been so successful that you can safely say

Terence in Switzerland, 1922.

that the only foreigners favourably received in the country are the Germans, who you meet in every town and village in scores.

Roumania is a country which is labouring under many difficulties, of which a few are: – its youth as a kingdom, its enormous increase in size since the war, its lack of an educated middle class, and thus of necessary officials for purpose of administration in the new countries, lack of transport, bad communication and corruption of the administration…

It is heartbreaking watching this wonderful country with all its potential wealth being gradually balkanised before ones eyes. Under Hungary it was perhaps 50 years behind, it is now quite 300 years behind and in another year it will be quite 600 years behind the times. The real trouble is there is no backbone to the country, the leaders of the Government set such a hopeless example. Honour, patriotism, all is surrendered to the acquisition of wealth. As soon as one political party has enriched themselves and their friends at the expense of the county, their political convictions dwindle, and in consequence they loose ground and are replaced by another party, who immediately repeat the process.

There is absolutely no hope for this country under Roumanian administration. I advise no one to invest money in it.

You cannot bolster up an effete and immoral race.

It is all very well from an armchair in England to talk about making allowances for them and giving them time and they will settle down. I thought so, at one time too; but now, on closer acquaintance, one realises the impossibility. Give them time or sufficient rope and they will no doubt hang themselves, but in so doing they will probably have spread red ruin all over Europe once again.

You can summon up the situation in Roumania to day in a few words: – As a struggle between Vienna culture in its broadest sense, i.e. German Kultur, of the new territories and the so called French culture of Bucharest, which is really a selection of all that is rotten and beastly of the French idea. However if the new territories manage to gain sufficient power politically to control the Government, you may safely say, that in course of time Roumania will be saved by being Germanised. Verily the spirits of Attila and his merry men would be consumed with envy if they could, but see to what perfection the art of destruction of civilised maxims had been brought.

I am afraid this destruction will bring this country to such a pass in such a short time that it will be too soon for the political power of the new territories to exert its self sufficiently to prevent the country being completely submerged in the muck heap into which it is now sinking.

What is so likeable about Max is his confidence; he knows he has a splendid future ahead. He frets because he doesn't altogether like his job, and yet he does it well. He is intelligent and he is liked. Charm is a meteorological entity. When a charming person enters a room the atmosphere brightens and tension is relieved. When the door opens to a dull person there is a numbness; it is as if a vapour fills the room, solid, like wadding. Nora filled people's lives with sunshine; Max filled them with energy and humour, increasingly with authority. He laughed and he could show his anger. People spoke of his 'presence.'

Nora had returned, and on 19 October 1921 their son was born, christened Terence Broke. The young couple spent some time in Switzerland with Terence and a nurse. We have wonderful pictures of Nora on skates and Terence on his sledge, with his black hair and naughty grin. Terence had the gift of charm. Max returned to England, disillusioned with his position and with the state of the world; this was truly the end of an era. He writes to his father on 14 January

1923 that the Labour government of 1923 is upsetting their financial status, though judging from the end of the letter they do not appear to be on the breadline. Nor did the young couple's happiness and fun last long. On 4 January 1924 Nora died in Switzerland of pneumonia due to complications after a skiing accident. In her memory Max gave skis to the schoolchildren of Adelboden. A letter from the Adelboden Ski Club in 1939 shows that this payment had been continued every year. The writer thanks Max, aware no doubt that the payment may discontinue upon the outbreak of war.

Postcheck-Konto
III 6966

Adelboden, den   March 8th, 1939.

Dear Captain Despard,

      The Committee and Members of the Adelboden Ski Club would like to express to you their sincere gratitude for the generous donation of ₺ 10 Sterling which you keep on sending to us year after year.

      This sum is regularly and fully being put into the special School Poor Childrens Fund. Every year this fund enables us to give a pair of new skis as a Christmas present to about 15 to 20 poor children who, otherwise, would never be in a position to enjoy this finest and healthiest of all winter sports.

      Needless to say that these poor children are always exceedingly pleased with your presents, and their genuine joy is probably the nicest reward for your extreme generosity.

      Hoping for the pleasure of seeing you in Adelboden again one of these days,

          Yours sincerely,

          ADELBODEN SKI CLUB

          per: *C. Lauber*

Lilanna Hurum, 1923.

Lilanna

Max was not to remain a widower for long.

My Norwegian grandparents were conservative in manner and politics. In Max's obituary my grandfather's name is given as 'J. Hurum, Esq.' In fact his name was Hans, but my grandmother preferred a French version and called him Jean, in Norwegian pronounced 'Shung.' They lived in a respectable area of Oslo, my grandfather did well in business and they owned a car very early. Grandfather was a passionate sailor and successful in ocean races. In the European Cup of 1914 he won first place, tied with Kaiser William.

The Hurum family originally came from Drammen and were successful in the timber industry. Their business included exporting pit-props to Cardiff, where one of the brothers was Honorary Consul. They were musical, not very tall, but neat with slanting blue eyes. In my grandmother's family Ording there were several notable scholars and teachers. This family also had fearless radicals, though closer to our time and involved in other battles than those of Colonel Despard. Johannes Ording was my grandmother's brother, godfather of Lilanna, my mother. He was a quiet man with a round face, far from athletic-looking. He was a theologian, as so many were in that family, and had a great sense of humour. He died young, broken down by Norway's famous 'Professorstrid,' the battle between theologians. In 1905 he had applied for, and was awarded, a Chair at the Faculty of Theology at the University of Oslo. His ability was not the main point of contention;

his doctrines were. His main heresy concerned the sacraments. He defined Communion as a symbolic meal. It is perhaps surprising that this should be anathema to Lutherans, but it was, and to conservative Norwegian Lutherans it was shocking that anyone might put such ideas in the heads of budding clergymen. The appointment triggered the founding in 1908 of the Norwegian School of Theology, Menighetsfakultetet, a conservative institution that has educated the majority of Norwegian clergy since the 1920s. The invective was harsh. The conflict became political and almost toppled the sitting government, and this at a time when Norway was negotiating its independence from Sweden.

Professor Ording married his cousin Fredrikke and they had three children, none of whom had offspring. His two sons were leading members of a group founded in 1921, to the left of the Norwegian Labour party, 'Mot Dag.' Its name (literally, 'Towards Day') is resonant of enthusiasm for the young Soviet Union. (Herbert Ernst Karl Frahm, later Willy Brandt and Chancellor of West Germany, was a member at one time while he lived in Norway.) By wartime many had readjusted their political convictions and moved towards the centre. Arne Ording, the older son, was close to the Norwegian government-in-exile in London and he became well known for his wartime reports. He was also known for his wit and insight. He was awarded a Chair in the Department of History at the University of Oslo. I only saw him once. He had then been bedridden for years with cerebral atrophy, cared for and turned in his bed by his wife and sister. Once he was seen fumbling for something on his bedside table. 'What are you looking for, Arne?' 'I'm looking for my lost brains.' In the five years Arne spent in London he never got in touch with his first cousin Lilanna, nor is she mentioned in his detailed war diaries. It is very likely that Max was not told much about this radical side of the family, nor would he have been very keen on his wife's left-wing relatives.

The Red House, Ula, circa 1920.

My mother Anna, called Lilanna, was born on 11 July 1903, and was followed by Hans Jørgen in 1906, Per in 1910 and Sven in 1912. The three brothers were gifted. Hans Jørgen became a leading music critic and Per a sculptor. Sven was a good singer and artist, but went into business and shipping, first in Manila, then in Montreal.

In 1920 the Hurum family bought a summer-house in Ula. At that time it was a long journey in the family's automobile, but only a few hours' sail south from Oslo in a good wind, exactly the time it took before the ice block for Hans's whisky melted. (In winter Ula was a major exporter of freshwater ice, even to America, but in winter the Hurums did not go there.)

147

Axel was the name of the chauffeur, a handsome man who doubled as crew. He was particular about appearances and even in summer told my mother that she had to wear stockings in the car. The family had spent their summers in Ula from the turn of the century, renting houses. Now the three most beautiful houses in the bay were bought up: the red house by Anna and Hans Hurum, the white house by Anna's brother Jørgen Ording, and the yellow house by Hans's brother Arthur, who had married Fredrikke Ording, Anna's sister, (not to be confused with their cousin Fredrikke who had married Johannes…). My grandmother Anna was an intelligent and strong woman, trained as a teacher. After the death of her husband and during the war she made her home in Ula. Ula and the Red House were to become a fixed point in the family life of Max and his descendants.

Lilanna must have been very different from the lively Nora. She was more composed. She was serious in her interests and had returned from her stay in Paris with a small library of French poetry. My mother was beautiful rather than pretty, but in a quiet way, not striking. She had perfectly regular features, narrow blue eyes and very fine, light brown wavy hair. There is something thoughtful and kind about her looks. She dressed very well.

The meeting between my father and mother has all the elements of popular romance. It took place at a ball at the royal palace. Queen Maud was the granddaughter of Queen Victoria and the youngest sister of George V. She married her first cousin, the Danish Prince Carl, and when he became King Haakon of Norway and she Queen Consort, she learnt skiing and worked hard at being Norwegian. However, she loved all things English and when the Royal Navy visited Norway she was undoubtedly pleased at the opportunity to meet British officers. The family Hurum was not especially grand, but my mother was sweet and good at languages and was taken up by the

Lilanna with (from left) her brothers Hans Jørgen, Per and Sven, 1916.

Queen. Hans Jørgen, Lilanna's younger brother, was a guardsman at the time and was proud of being ordered to deliver the invitation to his sister. Lilanna had sprained her foot and could not dance. However, a tall dark officer – my father – sat down with her. When she got home from the ball Lilanna told her mother that she had met the man she was going to marry.

I wonder how Max got on with my grandparents. They were typical bourgeoisie, whereas Max was used to the British outdoor upperclass life. He may have felt cramped in their flat, though it was large and elegant. I know he took care to drive up to Frognerseteren with Terence every day for lunch while my grandfather ate his 'fiskeboller.' Max could never stand 'pre-masticated food.' After the fishballs my grandfather would rest, having had a not always very strenuous day at the office. My grandparents had a sense of humour, indeed a great sense of fun. In Ula there was much jollity with processions in bathrobes and a lot of singing. Whether this was to Max's taste I cannot know. They were small and he was a very tall man; maybe they were rather overawed by him. However, he must have been very impressed by his father-in-law's sailing.

It must have been a feather in their cap that Lilanna had married this officer and that his best man was the Ambassador. However, there was the language barrier. Max made no effort whatsoever to learn Norwegian; he claimed that the only word he knew was *karbonadekaker* – meatballs. My grandmother Anna Hurum became resolutely anglophile. She went to every performance of the film of George Bernard Shaw's *Pygmalion* as there was a word she did not catch. The word was 'diaphragm.' When I was ten years old she and I solemnly celebrated Queen Elizabeth's coronation with lobster, sitting by her tiny radio. Earlier the intellectual tradition had been to look to Germany. Educated Norwegians read and spoke German,

Max on the beach at Ula, circa 1928.

some French and powerfully accented English. (Teddy Evans loved teasing Elsa, his 'Viking bride,' for her erratic English.) The academic orientation towards Germany persisted through the interwar years, though tempered by German submarine attacks on Norwegian shipping in the First World War. Although Norway was neutral, 1,400 merchant seamen drowned. After the Second World War and the Occupation of Norway, the attitude to Germans changed totally.

My parents were married in Frogner Kirke, Oslo, on 2 April 1925 at six o'clock in the evening. The wedding had been planned for 11 March, but the church register shows that the date was crossed out and replaced by the later date, with no explanation. The chief attendants were the Ambassador, Sir Francis O. Lindley, and Lilanna's friend Wenche Kallevig, known as Mossik. There was a celebration, but strangely enough we can find no photographs from their wedding. Was this because it was too short a time after Nora died?

Their happiness was not to last more than eight months.

Max (right) on the Harebell, 1925.

The *Harebell*

Lilanna was seasick all her life. Once she was sick into her new hat from Paris, and once she let a very small Anita fall from her berth without doing anything about it: she felt too ill. She married a sailor. She did not know that his seafaring life would soon be over. The *Broke* made Max's naval career; the *Harebell* undid it. In peacetime, on 30 November 1925, Max was on board the fishing patrol vessel *Harebell* when a gun exploded next to him. One man died, my father's hip was torn and his thigh filled with shrapnel. In his autobiography, Teddy Evans comments on the accident and understands its implications for Max's career:

> Taking my *Repulse* to Portland I had a sad experience, for it was here that I met Maximilian Despard lying in hospital, badly injured in a gun accident which had occurred in the *Harebell*. ...Despard's injuries left him unfit for active service for some time and spoiled his chance of early promotion, and, I fear, put an end to his promising career.

These are the facts recorded for the Admiralty:

CERTIFICATE FOR WOUNDS AND HURTS
    THESE ARE TO CERTIFY *the Right Honourable the Lords Commissioners of the Admiralty that Maximillian* [sic] *Carden Despard,*

Lieutenant–Commander, R.N. belonging to His Majesty's Ship *Hare-bell* being actually then upon His Majesty's Service *in being on board during gunlayers test was wounded on November 30th 1925 by the breech block of the foremost 12 pounder gun carrying away thereby causing: –a compound fracture of the left femur in the middle two thirds, associated with a large wound on the anterior and outer aspect of the thigh causing severe lacerations of the neighbouring muscles, (2) a dislocation of the distal phalanx of the left thumb, (3) a small cut over the left eye brow.*

He was *sober* at the time.

Age about *33* years. Born at *Stockport* Height *6ft 2 1/2 ins*. Hair – *dark brown* Eyes – *Brown* Complexion *Fresh*

Maybe they should have had his leg off, but he was terrified lest that would end his active career. I have also once heard that my mother, newly married, protested. We were not allowed to wear green in the family. I always thought this had to do with something Irish, but my sister tells me that my mother was wearing a green dress on the day of the accident.

Max was in hospital for many weeks, at first so critically hurt that all the men on the *Harebell* wanted to give blood to him. This was only a few years after 1909 when the Viennese Dr Karl Land-steiner had charted the various blood types, and now the men were queuing up to be tested. The *Daily Express* reported on 2 December 1925:

The condition of Lieut. Commander Despard, who was injured in Monday's gun explosion in the fishing protection cruiser Harebell, and is lying with three other of the injured men in the Royal Naval Hospital, Portland, is reported tonight to be critical.

Marjorie and Max at Ferneyhurst, 1926.

A transfusion of blood is to be made. And for this purpose the whole of the ship's company of the Harebell volunteered to pass the necessary test.

Sympathy poured in to Max, his parents and my mother from all quarters. My grandmother rushed from Norway to be with her daughter, even though she missed an important event, the confirmation of her second son Per. Max's mother came, his father was prevented. There is a letter from Jellicoe and one from Admiral Gerald Charles Dickens. He had been Max's captain on the *Glowworm* on the Danube, and was the grandson of Charles Dickens. We went to see him when I was a child and I can just remember him. He writes to Herbert John:

> It was good of you writing. You will have had the latest news from your wife. I had the pleasure of meeting her today. Your son seems to be doing better than we could have expected and we all have high hopes.
>
> Of course one always expects an officer to bear up well in a crisis, but Max' behaviour from the moment he was injured was in accordance with the very highest traditions of the Service. It couldn't have been excelled & I have brought his name for this to the notice of Their Lordships.
>
> Please excuse a hurried line but we have hundreds of wires & letters of sympathy to deal with – your son and the ship are very popular all round the coast.
>
> So sorry to hear you are laid up. I trust that continued good news of Max will soon put you to rights.

It is perhaps fortunate for us that Herbert John was ill at the time.

This means that we have all the letters which people wrote to keep him informed of Max's progress. This is Lilanna's letter to her father-in-law on 15 December. Her handwriting is clear and decisive, her English still a little wobbly:

Dearest Father,

It is very sad to hear you are so seedy. I hope you will soon be all right so you can come down here. Max had a **very bright** day today, the dressing had not been so painful so he was more rested and felt comfortable.

As it is more than a fortnight since the bad thing happened and Max is going on so well I think we ought to be quite sure about his leg and himself – don't you think so? My mother who has had a cold and not been able to see Max for 4 days found an enormous difference in him today, his appetite is so good, he had smoked two cigarettes today and had had whisky and soda 3 times – of course he just takes it as a medicine, he says!!!

The wheather here is bright but very very cold.

I do so hope you will recover quickly –

All my love to Mother and Terence.

Yours affectionate

Lilanna

Max was in pain for the rest of his life. From the time of the accident until his death in 1964, metal splinters travelled round his body, sometimes emerging. When he was operated on after the Second World War they found shreds of uniform attached to the bone. He always walked with a stick, he did not take painkillers and he rarely complained. I can remember sitting on his lap, but I cannot remember him ever telling me to be careful of not hurting his leg.

Lilanna and Max with Anita and Herbert in Finland, 1934.

Finland

If, if, if… If Max had stood closer to the explosion, the story would have ended here. If he had stood further away he might ultimately have retired on a comfortable admiral's pension. Or he could have been killed in the next war. These are fruitless speculations; what is certain is that the gun on the *Harebell* changed the course of Max's life. He wanted to go back into active service; now he had to change his plans.

First he needed to recover. In 1927 Max and Lilanna went on a tour of Europe by car. The journey was paid for by the Admiralty for Max to recover his health and return to active service after he had got his Interpreter's Certificate. Lilanna even took him to Lourdes. One of the written sources we have from the time after the accident is my mother's diary from their travels. The idea was that my father should recuperate in a warmer climate, and he was to learn French in order to embark on a new career. My father wrote to me once that his vocabulary was good, but his French accent appalling. My mother's excellent French was not commented on. (She had been enrolled at the Sorbonne in 1922, but her stay in Paris was cut short by the tragic and horrific death of her friend Ellen Hanson in a paternoster lift.) Like many travelogues, her diary does not make very interesting reading; it is impersonal and written as if to exercise her nearly perfect English. She mentions places, she writes about the car and she quotes her husband's opinions, whether these concern politics or poor service in hotels. She was only twenty-two at the time of the accident.

In October 1927 Maud Anita Lorne was born in Oslo, with Queen Maud as a godmother. She was a beautiful infant, plump with bright blue eyes and curly hair, but she did not charm Terence. He refused to include her in his prayers:

'God bless Mummy, Daddy, Grandfather, Granny, aunts, uncles, all kind friends.'

'But I didn't hear Anita,' said Grannie.

'Did you not hear, I said All kind friends. I have just put her in there. But now I am thinking how to put her out again.'

Terence was now living in Oslo with our Norwegian grandparents and Lilanna's brothers. He went there when he was four. Who decided where he was to live? It may be that my grandmother thought Lilanna was too young to be in charge of a stepson, or it may be that Max's accident changed everything. They all doted on the lively dark-eyed boy. And he was such an English gentleman. At the age of seven he was instructing his new grandmother on etiquette and how a gentleman should always walk on the outside of the pavement to protect the lady. He had been living with our paternal grandparents in Scotland and it would seem he was rather spoilt as he would only eat chicken and grapes. (This was also the diet of Margery's son Dennis.) Terence arrived with his governess Miss Smith, whom he teased. He was highly articulate for his age. Lindley said he dressed like a boy of seven and spoke like a man of forty. When Lilanna was getting ready for a picnic he asked why she needed so much 'paraphernalia.' He rapidly became bilingual. In Oslo he was one of the boys and in Ula he quickly became leader of a gang. He was spoilt and petted by his new grandmother and her sister Maja, and Lilanna's brothers loved playing with him.

Lilanna with Anita at the royal summer-house at Bygdøy, 1928.

It therefore came as a great shock to him when it was decided that he needed to become English and he was sent to prep school. All his life he spoke of this as the greatest betrayal. He had been happy in Norway, now he was on his own and unhappy. The discipline irked him and he was cold. He missed the lovely centrally heated Oslo home and he froze in the grim English school. He always liked being in opposition, creating his own alliances.

As to Max's career, it was inevitable that he would have to leave active service. His life as a naval officer was officially declared over in a letter of 27 June 1928: 'With reference to the survey held on you on the 20th June, 1928, I am instructed by My Lords Commissioners of the Admiralty to inform you that, as you were then found medically unfit for further service, they regret that it has become necessary to place you on the Retired List from that date.' He was thirty-six.

Max received many letters of sympathy and farewell letters to him as officer, such as the following:

I don't know that anyone could have had worse luck – except, I suppose, that you are lucky to be alive at all. I am so sorry – as sorry for the Service as for you since it means the loss of a very fine officer. However you are not the man to whine and I have very little doubt you and yours will find happiness some other way.

An extract from the report of the Commissioners points out his qualities:

Lieut.-Commander Despard. D.S.C.

By the retirement of Lieutenant Maximilian C. Despard, D.S.C., owing to ill-health, the Navy loses a gallant and most promising young officer. Unhappily he was seriously injured by a gun explosion

Terence and Anita with uncles and grandparents in Ula, 1928.

while serving as the Executive officer of the HAREBELL the Fishery Protective vessel, and his injuries have now resulted in his being invalided from the service. Promoted to Lieutenant during the first month of the war, he acted as gunnery officer in the Destroyer Leaders BROKE, SPENCER and ACTIVE; receiving the Distinguished Service Cross for his services in the action on the night of April 20–21, 1917 when as the "Gazette" stated, "he controlled gunfire and gave the orders which resulted in an enemy destroyer being torpedoed." After the war he served on the Danube International Commission, and was thanked for the manner in which he did his duty as representative of the Iron Gate section. In the following year he was Executive Officer of the GLOWWORM on the Danube, having been advanced to the rank of Lieutenant-Commander. The ability shown in diplomatic dealings with foreign officers was particularly noticed by his superiors. He was awarded the Portugese [*sic*] order of the Tower and the Sword, fourth class, and made a Chevalier of the order of the crown of Belgium.

Max had to find a new job. He needed every glowing letter of recommendation he had accumulated. In 1917 Evans had written of his zeal and that he had 'shown himself to be a very able first Lieutenant. I cannot speak too highly of his conduct in action or of his tact in dealing with the ship's conduct under very trying circumstances.' In 1925, before the *Harebell* accident, Evans wrote that he considered Max's service 'entirely to my satisfaction. A first class executive officer. Able, clever and handles men well. A good staff officer who would do well in higher rank.'

As British Delegate to the CID, Admiral Troubridge declared him in 1921 'to my entire satisfaction and has filled a most difficult position with great credit and ability.' Charles Dickens could hardly have invented a better name for a naval officer, but was Troubridge's letter the best recommendation? He was over sixty by now and recently retired. Moreover he was out of favour with the Admiralty. He had been a rear admiral on the outbreak of the First World War, but failed to engage two German warships in 1914. He was court-martialled, and though acquitted, his reputation was blighted. He died in 1926. (His second wife, the sculptor Una Vicenzo, was not much of an Admiralty wife; she left Troubridge for Marguerite Radclyffe-Hall.)

The First Lord of the Admiralty the Honourable Sir F.O. Lindley was surely a better bet. Moreover he knew Max well. When Ambassador in Oslo he had been his best man. He writes from Oslo in

October 1927, 'I may say that up to the time of his accident Despard proved himself to be an officer of exceptional ability, and will be considered for promotion when he is fit for service.' However, the Admiralty replies to Lindley, 'He is being re-surveyed this week, and if found fit for shore employment will be given an appointment.' Evans (now Rear Admiral) does his best to help Max in a letter of 7 July 1928 to the Clerk of the Standing Joint Committee, County of Leicestershire:

> The officer has been known to me for 11 years and I hold the highest opinion of him. He has any amount of personality and handles men, with a natural gift, to great advantage. He always gets the best work out of his subordinates and they like him.
>
> Despard is a clever fellow and would give his whole energies to his work, as he has always done in the past, to every appointment held by him.
>
> He rides well, and has a very distinguished war record, and is exceedingly good at administrative work.

Did he ever ride again? A month later Max passes an exam before the Civil Service Commissioners of the Admiralty and is awarded a Certificate as Acting Interpreter in French. In 1929 he got his next appointment, his first shore appointment. It was to Helsingfors, the Swedish name for Helsinki, as Naval Advisor to Finland. His responsibilities were not described as military or having anything to do with Finnish armament; he was responsible for 'Personnel.' His was a politically delicate situation. Finland had joined the League of Nations and was striving to become closer to the Scandinavian countries. However, the presence of Finland's large neighbour in the east made Sweden wary of too close a partnership with Finland. It was only the weakness of the new Bolshevik government that had made the Soviet Union recognize Finnish sovereignty in 1917. Yet Finland was a troubled nation. Relations between Russia and Finland had always been uneasy. They did not improve, despite the Soviet-Finnish non-aggression pact signed in 1932 and reaffirmed for ten years in 1934.

There were strong anti-Communist elements, although the Communist Party was banned in 1931. There was good reason not to trust Soviet Russia: the intention of the Molotov-Ribbentrop non-aggression pact of August 1939 was that Finland should fall into the Soviet sphere.

When Max was in Helsingfors, Finnish politics were lively. Politically the country was in turmoil in the interwar period. Like other Scandinavian countries Finland was extremely poor and divided along class lines. The city elite had little idea of the hardships endured by the poor in the countryside. Winters were harsh, harvests were poor and all too often people had to mix bark with flour in their bread. It was natural for workers and peasants to turn to the 'Reds' while the privileged defended the 'Whites.' Linguistic barriers on the whole followed this pattern of class division. When Finns meet Swedes or Danes now, the language is automatically English. At that time city dwellers and educated Finns spoke Swedish or were bilingual. Thus Lilanna had no problems, and Anita spoke Finnish-Swedish as one of her first languages. (I suspect that Max was a better linguist than he let on.)

The duties of Naval Advisor in a turbulent political climate cannot have been easy and it is to Max's credit that he coped so well. It is clear from the following report to the Admiralty from Ernest Rennie, the Minister in Helsingfors, on 30 May 1930 that he made a promising start:

Commander Despard assumed his duties here on April 1ˢᵗ 1929, his primary task being to assist the Commander-in-Chief in the work of reorganization of the "Personnel" of the Finnish Navy, a force that was in an embryonic and neglected condition. In addition to having to work in a country of bilingualism, he has had to treat with Naval Officers, who, though willing to learn possessed but scanty and elementary knowledge of service matters, & with military General Staff Officers, many of whom were still imbued with a certain 1918 mentality, & whose ideas as to Naval needs were, to say the least, nebulous. The difficulties that presented themselves in the accomplishment of his duties are accordingly evident.

It is fascinating to read between the lines. The next paragraph of the letter hints at the nature of the new Naval Advisor's work:

Not only are his relation with naval circles excellent and most friendly, but his more delicate connection with the Defence Authorities is such that he is treated with general confidence; the general scope of his duties is growing & becoming extended to wider questions, & his advice is slowly – for this is a country where matters do not move with undue celerity – bearing fruit.

Max is now moving into the 'nebulous' and 'delicate' territory in which he will be working for the next decade. Rennie diplomatically describes the slow pace of Finnish life and politics. It was just as well that Max had learnt patience in the Balkans. There was enough work for him. The Finnish Armed Forces had been practically non-existent on independence in 1919 and the country looked to Britain and Germany for help to rearm. Vickers-Armstrong supplied naval ships. Lancelot Leveson was their representative in Finland,

and through Max secured the contract with the Finnish government. Leveson and his wife kept in touch with our family afterwards and they arranged Anita's wedding reception in 1952. Anita says they were rather portly, but very good at dancing the rumba.

As Naval Advisor Max helped make arrangements with the Finnish authorities for the visits of British warships and other ceremonial occasions. He kept the Legation informed about naval matters and no doubt many other things also of a 'delicate' political nature. More importantly the Finnish navy was building up its own fleet, undoubtedly with the help of its British Naval Advisor. The British correspondent in Helsingfors reports: 'With the completion of the coast defence ship Väinämöinen, which has arrived in Helsingfors from Abo, where she was built by Messrs. Crichton and Vulcan, the new Finnish navy has received its first larger unit of modern type.' He goes on:

> In course of completion is a sister-ship the Ilmarinen, which was launched just a year ago. These ships are the result of collaboration between German, Swedish and Finnish naval experts, and special attention has been given to their suitability for the defence of the Finnish coast with its innumerable islands and skerries. Recently four submarines have been added to the Navy...Since April, 1929, the Finnish Navy has had the able assistance of Commander M.C. Despard, D.S.C., R.N., Naval Advisor to the Ministry of Defence.

I assume that the coastal defence recommended by Max was to protect the Finnish Baltic coast from Soviet ships. Terence told his son John that Max also contributed to building up the defences of Lake Ladoga, also against the Soviets. Though most of the Winter War of 1939–40 would be on skis in forest and frozen marshland

Anita and Herbert in Helsinki, probably in 1931.

rather than at sea, undoubtedly after five years Max must have contributed to building up the Finnish armed forces from a shaky start to a position of strength. Such strength that they could take on the Soviet Army – even though they would be fighting against the Soviets when they became our allies in the Second World War. Max would be fighting Fascism in the next war, but he was no lover of Communism, and his wariness was undoubtedly increased by working closely with Field Marshal Mannerheim.

In October 1929 Lilanna bore a son in Helsinki. He was christened Maximilian Herbert (still in the hopes of inheriting Charlotte's money from the late Maximilian Carden?). Life was pleasant for Max and his family. There was time for leisure and my father founded Finland's first golf club. The family lived in an elegant flat in Petersgatan 1C overlooking Brunsparken. The house is no longer there, but the area is still attractive. Anita had a Finnish-Russian nanny. Lilanna was careful not to let her take the children out at Eastertime, nervous that she might be carried away by the excesses of Orthodox worship. Later the children had a governess, Miss Heyhoe. She had been in the household of an aristocratic Russian family, and when they escaped after the 1917 Revolution she helped them by smuggling out diamonds sewn into her garments.

Lilanna's brother Per studied art in Helsingfors. He once tried to buy half a bottle of spirits and was told, 'Here in Finland there are no half bottles.' Lilanna moved in higher circles and in her diaries she notes parties, receptions, golf, dinner and teas – sometimes tedious. Max worked hard, and true to his kind he took his play equally seriously. Lilanna did her duty as a diplomatic wife and became a great favourite. She was also a favourite of Mannerheim. We had a photograph of him, splendid with white moustaches and a cloak, signed to his 'little white dove.' He lamented what a dull and sad place it was after they left. His politics have always interested me less than the fact that he called her a little dove.

Who was this distinguished visitor to Petersgatan? His life was colourful, though maybe not so very much more colourful than many great men of his time. Carl Gustaf Emil Mannerheim came from a distinguished but unhappy Swedish-speaking family and inherited the title of Baron. He was trained in the Russian Imperial Army and served in the Russo-Japanese war of 1904–5 on the Manchurian front. After the war he went on an expedition to Central Asia and China, purportedly an ethnographic

Anita and Herbert in Helsinki, 1932.

one, to look at the customs and tribes of the mountain regions. The real purpose was to gather intelligence for the Russian Army about the strength of the Qing Dynasty. Russia and Britain were both interested in Inner Asia – part of the 'Great Game.' The expedition was long and included being stoned by xenophobic Tibetan monks. While in Tashkent he met the Dalai Lama, trying already then to free Tibet from Chinese rule. He was handed a piece of white silk to give to the Tsar and in exchange he gave the Dalai Lama his Browning pistol, explaining how it could be loaded with seven bullets simultaneously – presumably to shoot oppressive Chinese.

Though Mannerheim made a distinguished career at the beginning of the First World War he resigned from the Russian Army after the Revolution of 1917. Or he was no longer wanted. When his own country declared her independence he returned to Finland. Though trained in the Russian Army and with two daughters by a Russian wife, he turned against Russia. He was bitterly opposed to the Bolsheviks and Communism and as Commander-in-Chief of the White Guards he fought the Red Guards with Germany's help in the Civil War of 1918. He was not happy about Finland's pro-German sympathy, but felt Germany was the lesser of two evils.

When Max and Lilanna first came to Helsingfors, Mannerheim worked for humanitarian causes, including the Finnish Red Cross and General Mannerheim's League for Child Welfare. He returned to public life and in 1931 was appointed Commander-in-Chief. From now on he spent his time reorganizing the army and seeing that the government allotted sufficient funds. He cultivated relations with Germany and Britain, hence his connection with Max Despard.

The Despards had left by the time Mannerheim faced his greatest difficulties. In the harsh Winter War of 1939–40 Mannerheim fought against the Soviets and in 1941–4 he was in command of Finnish forces fighting with the Germans. Churchill wrote a letter to him in 1941 before the war broke out saying how disappointed many of his British friends would be 'if Finland found herself in the dock with the guilty and defeated Nazis.' Mannerheim replied that he was sad to be in conflict with England, but he had to 'to safeguard my country…It was kind of you to send me a personal message in these trying days, and I have fully appreciated it.'

In honour of his seventy-fifth birthday in 1942 he was visited by Hitler. Mannerheim was embarrassed by the visit and tried to play it down. He disliked Hitler, not least for his diet: 'While the rest of us enjoyed the good but simple dishes, Hitler ate his vegetarian meal washed down with tea and water.' Mannerheim had no sympathy for Nazism but was forced into the alliance to defend his country against 'our hereditary enemy.' His loyalties must have been tested in many ways and to a great extent his story is that of many of his countrymen who turned to Germany. Finland was a deeply divided nation; in the Second World War brother could find himself fighting against brother. This part of Finnish history is still difficult; it is easier to commemorate the appalling hardships of the Winter War than it is to remember the Second World War, or the Continuation War as the Finns call it, fought against the Allies on the German side.

Mannerheim was made Field Marshal in 1942 and became President of Finland from 1944–6. His prestige was so great that his wartime role has to a large extent been left unquestioned. My mother once said to Mannerheim that she was frightened of someone. He told her never, ever to be frightened of anybody. Perhaps that was his secret.

In 1934, before he left Finland, Max was made Commander of the White Rose, an order established by Mannerheim, one of three official Finnish orders. The decorations on the order were originally

Lilanna in Helsinki, early 1930s.

designed by the great Finnish artist Akseli Gallen-Kallela. Max had already received Portuguese and Belgian orders, but weightiest was no doubt still the DSC from the *Broke* action.

The family stayed in Finland for five years. A farewell speech was made in honour of Max by the Representatives of the Naval Club:

> We wish to tell you, who during several years in our country has represented the British Empire's mighty Fleet, about our respect for you, and to thank you for the work performed by you during your time in Finland.
>
> You have witnessed the creation of the Finnish Fleet – and the help which you as an experienced Naval Officer has given us, has been of great importance to us.
>
> The Finnish People have not yet woken to the necessity for a Fleet as the safeguard of their livelihood and independence. It looked at the time as if all efforts for its development were in vain. Then came your help.
>
> With your clear insight of the conditions here and with your up-bringing in the influential British Empire you made a change in the outlook in the right direction and saved the existence of the Fleet.
>
> Now, as you are leaving us we ask you to bring our greetings to England. We ask you to put forth that we here in Finland hope for England's understanding in the work that we in the North perform for the defence of our country against the hundred years old enemy in the East.

There were lengthy farewell interviews in the main Finnish newspapers when they left. Translations into English were provided, as in the *Helsingen Sanomat* of 16 September 1934:

Captain M.C. Despard, who during 5 years has been attached as Naval expert to our Ministry of Defence leaves Finland after a few days. Capt. Despard has during these years got a large circle of acquaintances and by his winning manners has also won many friends. He has also had had an excellent occasion as a neutral party to give a statement of our conditions and especially that of the most important of our questions of defence, which he has followed closely.

When asked which defence measures a neutral state like Finland should concentrate on he has to weigh his words, but states unequivocally that he would recommend a strong air defence and smaller vessels to protect the existing larger vessels.

The interviewer of the *Uusi Suomi* of 16 September 1934 seems more interested in the personal than in personnel:

Air departments necessary for the coastal defence – Material of soldiers excellent, says Commander Despard in his farewell interview. – "It is difficult for me to leave this charming country" states he with humid eyes.

We rang yesterday at the door of Commander M.C. Despard in order to get a farewell interview with the English Naval Expert of our Naval Forces. Madame Despard opens the door and we are in the middle of troubles of moving. The house is full of men wrapping in cardboard the beautiful furniture and chests of drawers of the family. There is hardly anything else left than a little white chair on the balcony. It is offered to the interviewer but he as well as the person to be interviewed prefer to stand on the balcony towards Brunnsparken in speaking of the years Commander Despard has spent here. The sunny park of autumn is the best fond for this a little sad interview which took place yesterday morning.

I arrived in Finland in April 1929, states Commander Despard, and now, after about 5 ½ years I leave the country. And I am sorry to depart. He says it quite openly and his eyes are humid.

I have worked more especially in the coastal defence together with General Valve. I cannot speak of course of my work, as military matters are not talked of. But I may say that Finland has during her independence created a strong basis for her coastal defence. If the Defence Forces had had sufficient funds, the coastal defence could have been made quite excellent. The most important question at this moment is the organization of an aircraft department for the coastal defence. It is absolutely necessary.

Madame Despard had greeted us in fluent Swedish. "I speak myself also somewhat Swedish, says Commander Despard, but the Finnish language has been too difficult for me to learn. My wife on the contrary is of Norwegian origin. Therefore it has been easy for her to assimilate and she also is sad to leave. One of our children, the youngest son, is born in Finland and the 7 years' old girl is born in Norway. Both of them are at present staying with their grandmother in Norway. The oldest son is at school in England. Our children speak several languages. The youngest Swedish, the middle one Norwegian and the oldest English. They are charming children", says the happy father and shows us the photograph of the babies.

One of these babies must have been Terence, now at Eton.

Max is getting into his stride. He has had a grave setback; he is not the sailor in active service that he wanted to be. He has a job on land, but he is making the very best of it and succeeding well.

Max in Egypt, at the funeral of Fuad I, 1936.

Egypt

Suddenly I find myself holding a card, or photograph, of Max resplendent in his white naval uniform. He is wearing a mourning band and I think it must be for the funeral of Fuad I, who died on 28 April 1936. Fuad, the father of fat King Farouk, had substituted the title of King for Sultan when the United Kingdom granted Egypt nominal independence in 1922. Max's prominence in the funeral procession is an indication of the powerful British presence in the Middle East and the British and French hegemony over the Suez Canal that was to last until 1956. It had started in 1875 when Benjamin Disraeli by a stroke of genius bought up forty-four per cent of the Suez Canal shares. The canal was vital, saving shipping the long and hazardous journey round Africa. The gateway to India was secured. British rule was formalized in 1882 when Egypt became a British Protectorate.

We have always been told that wherever there was trouble, Max was sent. The Abyssinian Crisis was a diplomatic crisis resulting from the conflict between the Kingdom of Italy and the Empire of Ethiopia, then known in Europe as Abyssinia. Both Italy and Ethiopia were members of the League of Nations and as such had to adhere to rules of non-aggression between member states. However, Mussolini was intent on flexing his muscles and building an Italian empire in North Africa. In 1930 he built a fort at Walwal. In 1934 the garrison, guarded by Somalis, was attacked by a large Ethiopian force. The international response was to avoid war at all costs and to keep the League of Nations going.

In October 1935 the Italians invaded Abyssinia. The two nations were now at war. The League of Nations declared Italy the aggressor and now set about imposing sanctions. My father was sent to Egypt as Chief of Staff to the Senior British Naval Officer to keep an eye on how the sanctions were being imposed. To a certain extent they were. As Max writes to his father, 'The blockade is really biting now – tea is 6s a pound in Genoa.' However, this was not enough. The Navy's task was to supervise the traffic on the canal – but the League of Nations was half-hearted in its response and, fearing the outbreak of general war, nothing was done to block Italian access to the Suez. Max must have been furious at yet another decision made by lily-livered politicians.

Egypt was for Max a parenthesis and he did not stay there long. The political situation in Europe and the Middle East was becoming tense. Following Max in these trouble spots gives a feeling of déjà vu. Ethiopians and Somalis; his next challenge would again be Serbs and Croats. In March 1935 Max writes to his father from the beautiful city of Ishmaïlia on the west bank of the Suez Canal. His views on the political situation in Europe are interesting, no doubt coloured by his years in Finland:

…Europe is in a pretty chaotic state at the moment, but I am sure some good will come out of it. The French were stupid to make their pact with Russia, but I suppose they mistrusted us, but they knew definitely nearly a month ago what Hitler's reaction would be. We I suppose are to blame having reduced our armed forces to impotence and thus were of no use as an ally and no deterrent as a potential enemy. There is no doubt that we are inclining more and more to

180

the German viewpoint. I am sorry for the French, as I like them, but I am sure there can be no equilibrium in Europe without a balance of Powers. If Hitler should become friendly with Great Britain, who knows! He might become respectable? As after all one is judged by ones friends. A strong Germany but not too stong is essential and if she wants to blow off steam let her do it against bolshevism...

Colbury Manor in the late 1930s.

Colbury

I never lived there, I never went there, but the name Colbury is somehow magical to me. It was the place where Anita and Herbert had ridden their pony, the house where my family lived before I was born. I have lived in the same house now for thirty-five years. I own it, but it lacks the solidity of a house like Colbury, with its grey stone buildings and tall French windows.

When home from Finland Max had stayed with his sister Margery at her house Ferneyhurst, and he now rented Colbury Manor nearby, not far from Southampton. When Lilanna saw it she despaired; it was the last kind of house she wanted. After her luxurious heated Helsingfors flat, it felt gaunt and cold. Anita and Herbert always felt the house was not being properly used. This may have been because the master of the house was away so much. It may also have been that the house had previously been so full of life. It had been owned by the sisters Hony, five spinsters. In their time the gardens produced vegetables, fruit and flowers, the dairies were productive and the stables and coach-houses were all in use. One of the nieces of the Honys, Ida Gandy, wrote a delightful book called *Staying with the Aunts*, published in 1963.

'Tell me about Colbury,' I ask Herbert and he lights up. He makes sure that I record in detail the description of the house, the chickens, the greenhouse, the apple house with its slatted shelves that had to be scrubbed, the carrots kept in sand heaps and the potatoes in a straw clamp. This was a new world for Anita and Herbert, another England, country life they had never known. They went into cottages with no electricity, no sanitation, no running water. Their guide in this new world was Miss Crook. She took the children for walks in the New Forest and they were very fond of her. Miss Crook was a schoolmistress who owned a car, but she knew the old life. She told them about her father, old Tom Crook; when he was dying people came for miles around to listen to his death rattle. She lived near Colbury in a cottage in the way her grandparents had lived, with oil-lamps, a house pig, chickens and a well for water. There were fruit-trees and there was a parlour which was never used but which had some very good pieces of furniture. There was also a sword found in a chimney, dating from the time of Oliver Cromwell. She always had a side of bacon hanging in the kitchen. In those days they had a Pig Club, which meant that they only killed one pig at a time and shared between three families. Miss Crook also kept bees, and chickens she called fowls.

The Despard family lived the kind of life that was normal for their kind. There were maids and gardeners, there were dinner parties for the grown-ups, there was riding and there were tea parties. The governess, Miss Heyhoe, slept behind a screen in their room. The next room was a schoolroom and then came Terence's room. When the children woke up, the gardener had already lit a fire in their room. They had a pony called The Empress. And they were given their first puppy, Spot. Herbert and Anita went to dancing classes at Brockenhurst. Everyone went to church in those days, at least once on a Sunday, though the children were allowed to leave before the sermon. Much was Victorian, including the vicar. His name was Mr Thistle and he always wore a top hat as he walked about Eling visiting his parishioners.

Herbert and Anita's childhood seemed enviable to me. It was a proper childhood, healthy and well-disciplined and within the pale of the British Establishment. I had a brief glimpse of such a childhood

Terence, Anita and Herbert at Colbury, May 1937.

from Bartley, but lost sight of it. However, it lived on in my imagination, nurtured by the precepts of Arthur Ransome.

Terence had an allowance from his mother's property and spent his money mainly on tools and equipment for his workshop. He was eminently practical. Terence also paid Anita and Herbert for getting frogs to feed his grass snake. The family had a gamekeeper and Terence was deeply involved in everything that concerned game. When Max fetched him at Eton his luggage was carried out by three other boys. The largest piece was a rabbit net 100 metres long, for ferreting. Max may indeed have wondered whether his fees were being spent wisely. Terence may never have forgiven his parents for taking him from Norway and sending him to prep school in England, but Eton suited him better, there being some room for eccentricity and private enterprise. Terence was a good boxer and runner, but he did not apply himself to his academic work. Lilanna was always worried that he was throwing away his career prospects. Yet he was always busy. At school he conducted obscure transactions with locals, mainly involving ferrets. He kept a ferret in his room, not normal at a public school at the time. He was also the only boy at Eton to wear a shawl, one he had made himself.

Terence, Anita and Herbert were in Ula with Lilanna when Britain declared war on Germany at the beginning of September 1939. Herbert remembers his mother coming down to the pier to break the news with tears in her eyes. They were all somehow granted Norwegian passports and Terence, Anita, Herbert and Lilanna left Bergen by the *Stella Polaris* as soon as possible.

Colbury Manor, like Ferneyhurst, was dangerously near the docks at Southampton and was frequently subject to air raids. At Colbury they could see the docks burning from an upstairs window. Lilanna was working as a nurse, stationed in Totton. The house was filled with refugees from the bombing in Southampton. When the Union Cold Storage Plant was bombed and burnt the smell of roast mutton tantalized people for miles around. When I was a child I saw nothing but bomb-sites in Southampton and thought that was what towns were supposed to look like. During the bombing in 1940 the children were moved to 'safety' in the drawing-room, where they slept underneath a massive glass chandelier. There was a shelter where they were supposed to go, but they went into Lilanna's bed where she read to them. She read *Doctor Dolittle* while Southampton was bombed.

Herbert says that Spot the dog loved air raids and insisted each time on rushing round the rhododendron bushes looking for pheasants, thinking the raid was some kind of shooting party. Similarly, for Herbert and the boys at Eton the bombing was a matter of excitement and a hugely popular break in school routine. The children stayed at Colbury in their holidays and the house was kept on during the war, even when Max worked in Cardiff. Anita went back once to pick the apples. She went by herself on the train. Miss Crook did not think she should spend the night on her own in the house, but she did. She was only sixteen.

After Eton Terence took a course in farming and worked on a big farm near Winchester. He was nineteen when war broke out and he wished to join the Navy. While he was waiting for a ship he worked for a boat-building firm. The boat-builders made high-speed launches for the RAF to rescue airmen. Terence also acted as an air raid warden. He proved himself a brave and able fire-fighter, quick and decisive, putting out incendiary bombs on the roof and ending up with a whole case of partly burnt bombs which he had retrieved, mainly from the roof of Colbury.

Even before the war Max was away from home for long stretches. Lilanna seems to have coped extremely well. It is not easy to learn the English social codes, but she did. She certainly was very popular and she took her duties seriously, seeing to the children's education and social life. Perhaps she was too keen to learn the codes. Anita told me that Max once berated our mother for asking if someone was 'a gent.' Never was she to say such things, he told her angrily. He said she was not to teach the children such attitudes. From his letters Max seems quite a snob, but it cannot be pleasant to hear your own sentiments echoed or travestied. Max had been on ships and had lived among men of all stations.

'When did they sell Colbury?' I asked Herbert.

'They never owned it. People rented houses in those days.'

This was surprising to me, and explains much of Max's financial situation. He had never invested in property. Max never bought a house with his own money in his entire life.

Max with Anita and Herbert in Yugoslavia, 1938.

Romania

In 1938 Max returned to the Balkans. This is the most dramatic part of his story and marks the culmination of his career – for better or worse. The following chapter has been the most difficult to write. Max, the protagonist, is silent. He has left us with little written material and the accounts of what happened were partly destroyed or were long classified. It is a very confusing story. We have some available firsthand reports of the three parts of Max's time in the Balkans, books written by contemporaries of his. *One Man's War*, Michael Mason's privately published book from Romania, is surely the most exciting. Then there is Alexander Glen from Yugoslavia, and Maitland describing the journey out of Belgrade. There is also the account of the historian Elisabeth Barker, *British Policy in South-East Europe in the Second World War*. I assume that hers is the most accurate; it is certainly the least complimentary to Max. Maitland's book was written immediately after the war, when fresh in the writer's memory. Mason, privy to many secrets but not all, was published in 1966; Barker, who had access to archives, in 1976; and Glen, having correlated his own story with others who had been present, in 2002. I have found the sequence of events very difficult to follow, as the accounts overlap and partly contradict each other, and all is played out against the backdrop of tangled Balkan politics and internecine strife. One

Max at his desk. On the back of this photo he has written to Anita, "The best view in Vienna, with love from Daddy"

thing is clear: war was imminent, the Nazis were gaining power and Max was determined to do whatever he could to fight them.

He was appointed Naval Attaché to Belgrade and Bucharest, Acting Secretary General and Secretary General Designate of the Danube commission. His main office was first in Vienna, the headquarters of the commission and the political centre of the river. Anita and Herbert can remember a large dark flat. Max was virtually tone-deaf and they lived in Mozart Street.

Max was then posted to Orsova, a city he knew well. This appointment was to be very different from his first term on the Danube. Although he knew the country and the people, much had changed in nearly twenty years. He was older, no longer in active service and an experienced diplomat. Although the political climate had deteriorated, Orsova was a good place for the children to stay in their holidays. As late as in the summer of 1938 Lilanna, Anita and Herbert went to stay with Max in Romania, accompanied by their new governess, Miss Howe and travelling by motor car. Lilanna drove, even coping with the new autobahn, while Miss Howe sat in the front with her, reading the map. The children sat in the back in old-fashioned dustcoats, even though it was a modern saloon car. When my mother asked if there was a speed limit, she was told there was none for the British. They were well received everywhere and no animosity was shown to the English family.

However, when they drove into Vienna it was at the time of the *Anschluss* and the city was a Nazi stronghold. In German, *Anschluss* means 'link-up.' It is not clear how eager the Austrians were to come under Nazi rule. All nations continually rewrite their history and this can be painful. Certainly the 'link-up' of 12 March 1938 is still embarrassing to many Austrians, and it is doubtful whether Austria has altogether come to terms with her past. Whether they were compliant to the brusque visit from their neighbour or whether they were brutally invaded, the fact remains that the Treaty of Versailles had specifically prohibited a union of Austria and Germany. The Nazi 'all-German Reich' alarmed Britain and France, and yet no action was taken. On 14 March Prime Minister Neville Chamberlain stated in the House of Commons, 'The hard fact is that nothing could have arrested what has actually happened unless this country and other countries are prepared to use force.'

Hitler's annexation has been called the *Blumenkrieg*, or 'War of flowers.' Lilanna, Miss Howe and the children found the streets of Vienna garlanded and swastikaed and full of Brownshirts. Herbert says they went to buy an ice-cream and when all the children said 'Heil Hitler' on getting their cornets he and Anita wondered what they should say; perhaps 'God Save the King.' The shops had notices saying *Nicht Kaufen bei Juden* – 'Don't buy from Jews.' Anita remembers that Miss Howe taught them leather work and they needed to buy some leather. They found a shop that was closed and finally reluctantly opened to them. The Jewish shopkeeper was absolutely terrified, Anita said. Within a few days of the invasion 70,000 people had been arrested, and Jews sent off to concentration camps.

Had the Allied powers fully appreciated the strength of the Nazi forces? Hitler used the invasion of Austria to perfect his blitzkrieg tactics, and the next countries invaded were horrified by the speed in which the tanks thundered over their country under cover of the *Luftwaffe*. Stalin was still biding his time, expecting no aggression from Hitler after the signing of the non-aggression pact. He was not willing to listen to his informants and was resolutely unprepared for Operation Barbarossa and the German tanks hurtling over his own cornfields in June 1941.

The children and Lilanna stayed with Max in Orsova. Orsova is near the strategically crucial Iron Gates. The Danube narrows and there is a system of trains and canals and a pile-up of barges waiting to be navigated through. The children were unaware of Max's concerns. The family travelled on a steamer and they made trips on the Danube in the mahogany motor boat at Max's disposal. He took pictures of the children and, as Herbert says, they were out of focus in the foreground against detailed and perfect shots of the Iron Gates installations in the background. When the weather got very hot they all went to the lovely Lake Bled in Slovenia. There the children had their tonsils out. They both remember how primitive the countryside was, the peasants virtually serfs in fur hats and with their feet shod in rags. However, Romanian peasants traditionally wore thongs round their legs and feet and the children may have misinterpreted this. The Romanian peasants had already been granted many reforms and were very much better off than their Hungarian counterparts.

Lilanna visited Max both in Belgrade and Bucharest, and writes to her mother how much she preferred Bucharest, the Legation being so charming, the atmosphere lively and the food so excellent. Bucharest was a sophisticated and beautiful city, the 'little Paris of the East,' and in comparison Belgrade was drab. No doubt Lilanna found her feet; she had long been a diplomat's wife and she spoke good French.

Before Max took a house in Bucharest he stayed at the Athénée Palace Hotel. Even a modern guidebook recommends this five-star hotel, informing us that it was the decadent centre of the extremely rich Romanian upper bourgeoisie and aristocracy and was known, in later Soviet days, for its bugged rooms and honey-traps. In the 1930s it was the hotel where British, German and Italian spies all stayed, somehow coexisting. As Glen writes in *Target Danube*, the hotel combined 'both theatre and a cast of elegance and high drama. Old worlds and new were the players, spies of every persuasion spied upon...' Olivia Manning gives the hotel a central role in her *Balkan Trilogy*. I have seen the TV series, where the hotel provided glamour and opulent sleaziness.

I was lucky to get hold of Mason's book *One Man's War* – or, rather, pages of it that my nephew Richard, Terence's eldest son, patiently photocopied in the Imperial War Museum. This is his how Mason described the hotel:

The Upper-Class conspirators occupied the Athénée Palace Hotel; the Germans and Max Despard: so I moved in too, to be near Max. It was Swiss run and very civilized. We saw our opposite numbers

The Athénée Palace Hotel, late 1930s. Postcard sent from Lilanna to her mother, who collected stamps.

every day, when we lunched or dined there. Fellow we called 'Little Audrey,' who was a plump, smiling, unpleasant lowest-class Nazi with some organising capacity, but not very much. Naturally I found my belongings were searched almost daily, but as I had nothing for them to find I did not worry. They never pinched anything. I took care to get a room without any balcony to it, or near it. I didn't fancy night-intruders with daggers, and saw no reason to make things too easy for them. They tried eavesdropping, which got them nowhere, and spying through my keyhole, which cost one of them an eye. 'Little Audrey' and his thugs were not much credit to their profession.

When she wrote to her mother in Norway Lilanna did not dwell on the decadence of the Athénée nor its many forms of excitement. She merely said it was a lovely hotel, but rather expensive and that they must soon find a house of their own. The city certainly was beautiful, but it was a hotbed of intrigue and corruption. The Legation may well have been charming, but I'm not sure how well disposed they were to Max in the long run.

Max's sympathy lay with the Serbs. Lilanna may have enjoyed staying in Bucharest, but Max did not like the Romanians and had already in his first stay in the Balkans been exasperated by the 'mongrel race.' I asked a young Serb what her friends thought of Romanians. 'We feel sorry for them,' she said. And no wonder after the grotesque misrule of Ceausescu. Max seems to reflect the general British opinion at the time: that the people themselves were nice enough, but that centuries of being squeezed between Turks and Russians had made them unable to rule themselves sensibly. The aristocrats were few in number, rich and elegantly Francophile; the peasants were peasants and not as downtrodden as they might have been; but as to the middle class and bureaucracy the consensus is uniformly negative, in terms not acceptable in our time. Mason is blunt:

They are a strange mongrel people with a simple mongrel language. It is a very big and rich country; apart from its oil-fields it is a tremendously rich agricultural area, and the Danube itself – the greatest waterway in the world – would make any country rich. The enormous majority of the population is of simple Slav peasants – much the same as the peasantry in Russia, Ukraine, Bessarabia and Poland. They can't read or write, they don't know what is going on, and they probably do what they are told. They have the quality of good cannon-fodder, [....] The aristocracy is so small it counts for little. They are detached from serious matters (from the little I have seen of them) and their spiritual home is Paris.

The middle class – and a rich country like Rumania has a big powerful middle class – were the real super-mongrels of all the rabble of all the countries within a thousand miles, all mixed up in a curiously unquarrelsome hotch-potch. [....] Someone described Rumanian men as: 'Walking down the street, they are obviously on their way from their mistress to their venereal specialist, or from their venereal specialist to their mistress.' They do have a sort of bewildered, disillusioned look, and it always seems that nothing really matters much, and nothing whatever is worth the risk of bodily harm by such violence as warfare.

Whatever Mason thought about the Romanians, he knew how to get on with them and how to charm the 'Rumanian office-wallahs:'

As time went on I had more to do with Rumanians of importance, and found that patience and politeness got me what I wanted better than anything. The Germans – and the country was swarming with Germans – would shout at these Rumanian office-wallahs, and threaten, and bang the table so that the ink was upset, and generally behave like hogs. These people were frightened of them, but they hated them very deeply. So I took the opposite line and was very polite and accommodating, content to talk trivialities for half-an-hour before coming to the point. Also my French was much better than their own, and when I talk French I naturally use French gestures. They greatly admire the French and try to copy them. So they found me a most agreeable fellow. And when they learned, increasingly as time went on, that the Germans were frightened of me, I became more popular than ever with them – although I brought them up against more problems.

The countries were not yet at war, but the situation was tense, despite the restaurants and good life. Lilanna writes to her mother in the winter that Max is getting fat. She says he is not getting enough exercise as he is afraid of slipping on the ice with his bad leg. Max was athletic and good at most sports. He also loved good food and good company. It is from other sources that we become aware of the pain he was suffering. Lilanna's letters are full of detail, but are naturally guarded as to Max's work. It is highly unlikely that she knew all his activities, apart from the formal and social events that take up much of a diplomat's time. She was there again in 1939. Norway was occupied from 9 April 1940. In her letters to her mother I cannot see that Lilanna mentions Finland, but she does several times express severe disappointment with Sweden for its neutrality: 'I cannot understand Sweden!' she writes. Not only was Sweden neutral, but Sweden allowed iron ore to be shipped out in neutral ships to feed the German war machine. In recent years the passage through Sweden of German troop trains has also come to light.

The Balkans were, as the Balkans are, a mesh of ancient strife and intrigue. This meant that when war came, the Serbs joined the Allies, while Bulgaria turned to the Axis powers. What Romania would do was not clear. Which side in which country should the British trust? In Yugoslavia the Serbs were in the good books of the Allies, having fought so bravely on their side in the war. However, Romania was another story. It would seem they had less to fear from the Germans than from their great neighbour to the east. They feared the Soviet Republic that was casting its eyes on the riches of Romania, its land, minerals and oil. The German-Soviet pact confused the issue. The Balkan countries were caught in a pincer. As time went on, the Germans skilfully pitted one side against another, though they were not interested in open conflict. The non-aggression pact was a shallow alliance. The two powers glared at each other in the months before the war and it seems extraordinary that Stalin could ignore what was becoming open strife.

So the Romanians sat on the fence, keeping on as good terms as possible with the British and French while allowing the Germans to make inroads. Max had observed twenty years earlier that the Germans were everywhere 'in scores.' Glen finds it surprising that British Intelligence and the many British working in the Romanian oil companies were not aware of what was going on. The enemy was formidable. The Abwehr, the German military intelligence, was led by the brilliant Admiral Canaris. He was celebrated as a submarine captain and much decorated hero of the First World War, and quickly rose to prominence. However, he was no true Nazi and was involved in several attempts at a coup before the plot of July 1944. He was arrested, but not immediately executed as were so many officers, or told to end his life, as was Rommel. Hitler wished to learn his secrets. He met his end in Flossenburg concentration camp, where he, Pastor Dietrich Bonhoeffer and others were made to walk barefoot and naked to the gallows. His secrets are not yet known and maybe it will never be known how much he collaborated with British Intelligence. Such was the enemy, also unto its own. What did the British do about it? Barker is not impressed:

The story of Britain's relations with South-East Europe during the Second World War was for the most part a story of last-minute improvisation and the undertaking of commitments without the resources to fill them. Policies, if that is the right name for them, were largely dictated by negative outside factors: first fear of annoying Mussolini, then fear of provoking Hitler prematurely, after that fear of irritating Stalin; there was later the wish to avoid trouble with nagging exiled governments.

The British had various kinds of operation in mind. First there were operations to be carried out before war broke out while the country – i.e. Romania – was still neutral. Some of these were planned as fairly large-scale operations which entailed a considerable risk of annoying the enemy and causing an earlier outbreak of war. However, occupation was inevitable and the SOE, or Special Operations Executive, was also responsible for planning to undertake subversive and covert operations in enemy-occupied country, whether short, sharp exercises or operations of long-term duration.

Agents were sent to Romania to carry out sabotage. We shall never know the full story of Max's involvement or how important he was. Records were destroyed. We know Max sent for Mason and we know that Glen was sent to work for him. We can read from their narratives that he was central to certain operations and, if not a prime mover, then certainly privy to much that was going on. We do know that he was in close contact with Section D. Part of the many-headed secret service, Section D had been set up in 1938 to look into secret offensives and the many different ways in which an enemy could be attacked on the spot. London was masterminding the plans.

The story of the secret services is long and complex with bewildering acronyms and rival departments in Whitehall. Military intelligence – MI5 – was under the Home Office and its aim was to preserve secrets at home. MI6 was under the Foreign Office and its job was to work abroad. M.R.D. Foot has written an account of the SOE in his book *An Outline History of the Special Operations Executive 1940–1946*. He writes that in the first months of the war 'lethargy had been the characteristic of the government's handling of affairs. Winston Churchill changed all that.' Churchill understood that there was resistance in every occupied country and that these countries were looking to Britain. Section D was small and in July 1940 it was amalgamated into the SOE with MI(R) (R for Research). The SOE was formed in June 1940, the 'ministry of ungentlemanly warfare' as Churchill called it. Although Whitehall and many of the departments were full of intrigue and rivalry that hampered and obstructed action, the Admiralty was not one of these. The Naval Intelligence Division, or NID, was quick to recruit capable agents and send them off with such mandates as 'Cause havoc on the Danube.'

Many of the agents were refugees from occupied countries preparing to return on missions. The British agents were most carefully recruited from all walks of life, though there was undoubtedly a majority of public school men. In country houses these people learnt secrecy and forgery, the dismantling and reassembling of small arms, and silent killing. The story was that agents had potassium cyanide capsules drilled into their wisdom teeth. I have always wondered how this was possible. What happened if they bit into an apple or a hard piece of bread? I asked a dentist who suggested that the only way to conceal a capsule, however small, would be to cap one of the teeth and make a cavity large enough for the purpose. Googling the question is not enlightening; there are lurid stories of top Nazi suicides, but nothing of British or Norwegian agents who would have been equipped with such means of avoiding torture and betrayal of others.

One of the operations that had horrendous consequences was the assassination of Richard Heydrich, Reichsprotektor in Prague, in September 1941. The two agents had been ordered not to involve anyone else, but they did, and this third party gave them away. The two managed to kill themselves, but in the pocket of one of them was the name of two villages, Lesaky and Lidice. The revenge was terrible: the villages were both razed to the ground and all the adult inhabitants were killed, as were most of the children. Nine children survived from Lidice. The gains of sabotage had always to be weighed against the inevitable repercussions of the terror regime.

One of the most successful operations of the SOE was the sabotage in 1943 of the hydroelectric plant at Rjukan in Norway, carried out by Norwegians dropped in the mountains by parachute. Not only did the Norwegian agents under Captain Martin Linge carry out the sabotage with minimal loss of life, but they destroyed a vital supply of heavy water and effectively prevented a Nazi atomic bomb. Foot speaks highly of the Norwegian resistance and the toughness of the agents. At the end of the war 365,000 German troops were disarmed by fewer than 60,000 men and boys in woollen stockings and knickerbockers, armed by the SOE.

Early in the war while Romania and Yugoslavia were still neutral, there was room for officers and diplomats with imagination and 'wide duties.' In the Balkans the Danube was the main target for sabotage. It was the main waterway for food from the rich Romanian countryside and for Yugoslavian mining products. Above all there was oil, oil carried on the barges of Shell, the biggest fleet on the river. Germany was dependent on oil. The German army was entirely mechanized; the whole success of its blitzkrieg tactics was due to its hundreds of airplanes and its thousands of swift well-fuelled tanks. Lilanna's brother Hans Jørgen was in France in 1940 and describes how unaware the French were of German strength and efficiency. When the German army attacked France the French consoled themselves with the notion that the enemy would eventually run out of fuel, and perhaps try to fill up their tanks at local petrol stations. Not so; the army brought with it massive cylinders of the precious fuel.

Most of the oil came from Romania and Russia. The Romanian oilfield at Ploesti was a main supplier and the Danube was the route. None of this was news. When in late 1916 the Romanians came onto the side of the Allies, the German response was to capture the oil-fields. However, a British destruction team got the reluctant permission of the Romanian government to destroy the oil wells. The sappers did such a thorough job that the production of oil was entirely stopped. How could this supply be stemmed two decades later when there was a substantial and powerful German force already present in the region?

These matters are perhaps most clearly seen with hindsight and through the sober eyes of Barker. She is not impressed by British sabotage. Writing with access to Foreign Office archives she sums up the different British attempts:

It was in the field of destruction and sabotage that the British showed lack of experience, though plenty of enterprise and enthusiasm, sometimes too much. In the case of Rumanian oil, both section D and M.I.(R) were involved, and also the Director of Naval Intelligence. In the summer of 1939 M.I.(R) drew up destruction plans. George Taylor, though belonging to Section D, not M.I.(R), took the plans to Bucharest and handed them to the Rumanian General Staff in the hope that the Rumanians would put them into practice in the event of German invasion. […] The Germans however were watching. As early as December 1939, according to the British Air Attaché in Bucharest, a German broadcast showed that 'the Germans are well acquainted with our oil destruction plan…they disclosed the exact number of men involved'. In any case, as the Foreign Office later put it, the British destruction plans seemed 'doomed to failure': 'when the time came the Rumanian authorities refused to act and put military guards round the wells and refineries to prevent any action by British agents.'

There were many plans and several approaches to destroying the oilfields: bombing was one. The most radical and clearly the most efficient means of attack would be to bomb the oilfields and stop the flow of oil at the source. This was advocated, indeed urged, but for many reasons was not carried out until August 1943, when American planes took off from Benghazi in Libya. The daring air raids on the refinery – Operation Tidal Wave – have been duly celebrated; they were tragic in loss of life, but unfortunately barely effective in reducing the output of oil. The first bombs that successfully hit the oil wells in 1944 were Russian. These air raids do not form part of our story, as Max had left by then.

In June 1940 a plan was hatched in London to go to the source and destroy the oil wells. The idea was to cap the wells with quick-setting cement and steel plates. This was never carried out as the Abwehr were all too aware of the plans. The British oil companies had recruited large numbers of new personnel, but, as Glen writes: 'The Head of the Abwehr in Bucharest was not hoodwinked; he thought that the new arrivals looked more like British officers in plain clothes than oil technicians. Their free use of money in Bucharest gave him the impression that these men belonged to the Secret Service.' He reported them to the Romanian secret police. From then on the Romanians expelled all British personnel, and the Abwehr waited for German technicians to take over. In many ways this had been long due. The historian Jardar Seim has charted the rise of Fascism in eastern Europe, attributing the growth of the Iron Guard (*Garda de fier*) to fear of Communism and a particularly Romanian brand of nationalism and religion. The Guard had been hunted down by King Carol, but after the king abdicated in 1940 they were back in power. Maitland tells us of the harassment of British engineers and citizens, one example of the Guard's reign of terror:

The terror now began in earnest. Five British subjects, four men and the wife of one of them, were arrested by the Guards in Bucharest, whisked away to be tortured. They were experts from the oilfields and for two days their whereabouts were a mystery. Then at last we learnt they were in the hands of the police and had been maltreated. The police said they had been handed to their custody by "civilians" who had furnished proof in the form of signed "confessions" that they were guilty of "intended sabotage".

All major operations failed. The British underestimated the intelligence and the amount of preparation of the Germans, and they relied on the Romanians, who were not to be relied upon. What did succeed were the 'short sharp exercises' carried out by agents such as Mason, alias David Field. He says that he kept many of his exploits secret from Max, though others were no doubt encouraged by him. My father had to respect his diplomatic status, but it was, after all, he who had recruited Mason, and the two worked closely together.

In his book, Mason describes how he was recruited to join my father in 1940. Not for the first time, he was called to the flat of Reginald Hall. Known as 'Blinker' because of a facial tic – caused, his daughter suggested, by malnutrition suffered at a military school in his childhood – Hall had been British Director of Naval Intelligence, but that was in the last war. He had a long and distinguished career behind him and was perhaps best known for establishing the Royal Navy's code-breaking operation, Room 40. One of his achievements was in the decoding of the Zimmermann Telegram; another was intercepting the steamer *Aud*, carrying German arms to Ireland in 1916. He was also involved in the arrest of Sir Roger Casement. However, all this was in the past and his efforts in the Second World War were supposedly limited to the Home Guard. In reality he pulled strings behind the scenes, and according to Mason, even Admiral John Godfrey, the Director of the NID, came to him for advice. Hall's wife was sent out, as she always was when Mason visited. This time Mason was shown a letter from my father requesting a person to carry out work he cannot undertake himself. This is how Hall presents the mission:

'Another job, Mason. Danube. Biggest hole in the blockade of Germany. Oil from Rumania and Russia. Want you to go and block up the whole thing. Despard out there. Diplomatic, so needs help. Show you his letter.'

He handed me a letter which ended up:

'So you see I really need a clever, reliable man who can do all the things which, as a member of the C.D., I cannot do! In fact, I want a perfectly ruthless thug whom I can like and trust, and if he talks the King's English so much the better.

Yrs. Max D.

P.S. for Christ's sake don't send me a bloody pansy!'

'Despard? He was Evans's First Lieutenant in the *Broke*. D.S.C. Got blown up by a gun after the war. Crippled ever since. Clever man. Irish. Some people think he's too clever, so they are frightened of him.'

All of Mason's book is written in the same brisk style as the above. Mason said he had been praised by Kipling for his prose, and urged by Kipling he wrote many spirited books of travel and adventure. Yet *One Man's War* was published privately and handed only to some of his friends. In 1966 a secret was still secret. I think another reason for publishing privately might be his sprightly descriptions of named persons. Fortunately, he is full of admiration for my father:

Captain Max Despard was an enormous man of commanding appearance and a very charming manner. Irish-Huguenot, tremendous force of character, very good company, very economical with the truth. His wife said to me, long afterwards: 'Max has been so long in Secret Service that he's practically incapable of telling the truth about anything. It doesn't worry me or affect our married life. After all, he was that way already when I first met him.'

Terribly crippled by a gun-explosion after the First War, Max had been on Naval Attaché jobs ever since. There was probably no better brain in the Navy.

The oil wells had not been destroyed. The only thing that could be done was to hinder or block German transport of the oil. This was Mason's *métier*. When it came to action, Mason had his 'Man Friday,' Blackley, a skilled engineer from Clydeside:

Extraordinary chap: he attached himself to me like a dog. As he had been a rating in the previous war he revered Captains R.N. like Despard, and was too frightened of him – but he had one fixed idea: to destroy these bloody Germans. [....] All he cared about – beyond killing Germans – was women and drink. He took women as they came – and they were all alike to him – and drank like a fire-engine, with no effect beyond giving him an increased feeling of well-being.

Mason and Blackley set to work to do whatever they could to hinder traffic on the Danube. Mason was instructed to do everything in his power and by any means to stop the oil reaching its destination. He describes the harassment of Germans that was being carried out well before the outbreak of hostilities:

Michael Mason, alias David Field, circa 1945.

Constanza. There were Russian ships coming in all the time, from Batum, laden with lub-oil. Rumanian oil makes fine petrol but there is not enough lubricating oil left in the residue. So they had to have it from Russia. It all went, over the railways or up the Danube, into Germany.

The first thing, which I did not invent myself, was wrecking trains going into Germany. Naturally we chose places where they had to stop just before the steep pull over the Carpathian Mountains. All we did (Blackley and I) was run about in the dark, pouring acid into the axle-boxes of the trucks. Then various forms of wreckage happened. At the least degree the truck seized up or caught fire on the way up-hill and the line was jammed. At the best the whole train dived in ruin down a mountainside as it rocked its way down the far slope. It wasn't very much, but it irritated the Germans because they lost trainloads of lub-oil from Russia, or of petrol from Ploesti. What it meant to the Rumanians was of no matter to us. Fortunately they are people who take other people's troubles lightly.

He poured acid into the axle boxes of trains, he fastened limpet mines on oil carriers. He worked alone or with the help of local people, including a 15-year-old Greek schoolgirl who carried mines in her satchel. As this was still before a declaration of war the German and British agents were still living in the same hotel and had somehow worked out a *modus vivendi*. It is difficult not to include entire chapters of Mason's book; the style is irresistible. More and more Mason irritated 'Little Audrey,' the local head of Gestapo. Mason amused himself by goading him. Mason was shadowed, often in an exceedingly clumsy manner. He shot some of his German shadows in broad daylight. Once he threw two of them head first out of the Orient Express. (This is one of the exploits another man was to lay claim to.) There was a high price on Mason's head. No wonder: he alone blew up the vessel that was the headquarters of German surveillance of the Danube:

Many of the top planners lived together on this boat. To get the whole lot in one bang was a fairly obvious move, so three limpet bombs, one loaded with highly incendiary matter, were got ready and synchronised.

On the general principle that the fewer the stalkers, the better the sport, I did the job alone. It involved a good deal of swimming and wading, for at that time the limpets were of strong magnets and too heavy to swim with more than one at a time. But I got them well planted, the incendiary against the engine room. Then I waited, shivering in the sandy-muddy water under the bank. The water was beastly cold. The bangs went off nicely; ten seconds would have covered the three. I was waiting to make sure no-one came out alive. Blackley, who was no great swimmer, was keeping guard above, against shore interference.

Only three men swam ashore, for the vessel was a sinking furnace within a few moments. I shot the first man through the head; then my Luger pistol jammed, from mud and sand, and I used it as a club to brain Chappie No. 2. He sank, too, but the sharp, claw-like foresight (of the Luger) gouged a chunk of flesh clean out of the palm of my right hand. With a muted curse, I flung the pistol aside and Chappie No. 3 got the full force of my ill-temper. I grabbed him by the neck and strangled him under water...

Mason carried out much of his thuggery on his own, but Max was his boss and they worked closely together:

Blackley was at that time 'Engineer Inspector' of the English-owned fleet of Danube tugs and barges. At the time I got there all these vessels were ice-bound, but Despard had plans for them when the river opened, and I was made a sort of general O.C. Danube Shipping. I saw all the ships and the skippers and engineers, and learned the general form. Naturally the most interesting part was the Iron Gates, where the river comes through a narrow gorge, and towing strings of barges up is an art that takes a bold pilot eight years to learn.

Day by day, when I was back in Buchurest, which was my H.Q., Max Despard told me more and more as he got confidence in me. It was against his nature and *métier* to have confidence in anyone, or tell anyone the truth, but I was the man who was to put his plans into practical shape and carry them out. As time went on an increasing friendship grew up between us...[....]

His Britannic Majesty's etc., etc., in Buchurest, was Sir Rex Hoare. He sent for me one day. Wanted to know what I was doing. I was cagey. After all, I wasn't under his orders, although in another way I was. So whenever he wanted to know what devilries I was planning to do, I used to tell him what I had already done a week or two before. He would firmly forbid me to do it. I would say, 'Very good, Sir.' He never found out anything that was going on.

The following passage describes the most successful of the schemes to hinder transport of oil on the river:

I can't remember whether it was Max or myself who hit on the pilots as a vulnerable link. Anyway, with very little trouble, beyond a few days of hard work on the river, I managed to detach all the pilots of the German fleet on the lower river from their allegiance and engage them on full wages myself. They were to be paid for having a lovely long holiday. They were mostly Greeks; a poor lot on the whole. What a yell went up from Brother Boche! Even the Minister heard about it. Wanted to know what we were going to do next.

Max answered: 'When we've stopped laughing we are going to do the same in the Iron Gates.'

Now that was a tougher proposition. The Germans and the Austrians had about thirty pilots of their own on that stretch. Two were Austrians, who were ruled out. Six were Hungarians, who were doubtful. The rest were Yugo-Slav, Rumanian and Bulgarian. For these I needed a lot of money and a very great deal of persuasion.

He wrote for money, but in 'London they dithered!' It was urgent to get enough money quickly before the ice broke on the river. So he wrote a letter with a 'good deal of rough language' which Churchill ordered be read out verbatim at the next War Cabinet meeting. Churchill was keen to cut through red tape and was an advocate of unorthodox methods. Mason was awarded £50,000. 'Actually I did the whole thing for just over £7,000.'

What a time that was! Three days and nights arguing with thirty shouting men, in about five languages. I used bribery, threats, and most of all a dreadful imagery depicting those men's wives and daughters raped, the pregnant ones ripped open, the babies roasting on German bayonets. It seems like a vague nightmare now, but I got them all away and shipped them to Palestine and Egypt on one-way tickets – with words passed elsewhere not let them come back. So now Brother Boche was without pilots from the Black Sea to Orsova above the Iron Gates. He was not pleased! An Iron Gates pilot takes eight years to learn his job. What they did in summer, of course, was to bring in Rhine pilots and North Sea sailors, but these did not know the river, and string after string of barges and tugs were swept to ruin in the Iron Gates.

The tugboat scheme was highly successful in reducing the German deliveries of oil. Now there was another plan, the maddest and one favoured by Max. Not only by Max. Glen writes that Section D, later absorbed into the SOE, did favour 'Despard's Hornblower style exploit.' There had been many large operations planned and set afoot. Glen tells us of field force raids mounted in late 1939. These failed due to the vigilance of the German intelligence and the vacillating policies of the Romanians; rather, policies that became less vacillating and more pro-German as time went on. Glen says that King Carol himself was active in passing British plans on to the Germans. The accounts of these plans are bewildering, at times contradictory. I will therefore limit myself to those ventures where Max is specifically mentioned, such as that of the SS *Mardinian*, described by Glen at length:

In those dire days of Spring 1940, a major naval venture against the Danube was perhaps the last thing one might expect. Despard, however, had certainly not forgotten the years of the First World War when British gunboats, such as HMS *Ladybird* and HMS *Gnat*, ruled the Danube and even snatched to safety the last empress of the Austro-Hungarian Empire from the Red forces of Bela Kun. Whether Section D remembered those great days is not known, but they shared Despard's determination for a Hornblower-style exploit.

On 29 March the SS *Mardinian*, out of Liverpool, berthed at Sulina. She carried 68 Royal Navy officers and ratings, with Commander A.P.Gibson, RN, in overall command and cargo, including 65 cases invoiced as Chrysler spares and addressed to their agent in Bucharest. The Royal Navy personnel were immediately dispersed, contrary to Romanian regulations, into river craft. Customs cleared the cargo, encouraged by the £1,500 'sweetener' provided by Despard, which was then handed on to a group with a distinctly non-Romanian but rather an RN look, including a certain Michael Mason. [This cargo ended up in Giurgiu in the hands of the Romanian customs officials who were badly paid and, by then, effectively in the hands of the Germans. As Glen says:] It did not help that one of the cases still had attached the official label, 'Demolition explosives'.

There followed a complex struggle between sympathetic officials in Bucharest and their pro-German subordinate officers in Giurgiu. This only ended when Fabricius, the German Minister in Bucharest, overcame the helpful obstinacy of Gafencu, Romania's Foreign Minister, by threatening to stop further delivery of arms from Germany to Romania if the flotilla was allowed to proceed. This argument was referred to King Carol and, not surprisingly, the King decided in favour of Germany.

Was the plan foolhardy and unrealistic in itself? Was Max being gung-ho? Glen certainly implies this, yet he also makes clear that London was too late in estimating the strength of the German presence on the Danube. The British and Romanians had signed a plan to deny oil to Germany, but the Germans were ahead. Plain-clothes soldiers had long been there in full force, employees of the so-called Danube Shipping Company. Near the Iron Gates were sports clubs whose numerous members had been seen vigorously rowing since 1938. The Abwehr also had close links to the Romanian Siguranta, the secret police which was no less unsavoury in those days when they hunted Communists, Jews and Hungarians than they were later as Securitate, the instrument of Ceausescu.

It is hard to know whether the following venture described by Mason is the same or another. It is dramatic enough:

Max Despard had a scheme to bring the Germans down the Danube, with guns firing. This would bring the Rumanians automatically into the war on our side. That would enable our Army people to destroy Ploesti, which could not be done without their connivance, for they had it better guarded than the President of the United States; guards, machine-guns, police dogs. Our little handful of soldiers-dressed-as-clerks could do nothing without their agreement. So Max had planned to arm all our tug-boats and tug-barges – anything that could go under its own power, and simply go filibustering up the river from Rumania towards Austria.

Obviously, with the small guns we could erect on light river-boats, we would be blown out of the water. Equally obviously we would not get far before that happened. On such information as we had we believed there were German river gun-boats and military aircraft in Vienna.

The Rumanians believed that if they were invaded they could hold out for six months, and that by that time we could come to their aid with adequate force. Naturally our side encouraged that belief, though none of us believed for a moment they would last six days. But less than six days would be enough to blow up the oil-wells and refineries. What happened to Rumania after that I fear we did not care very much.

Max had arranged with Admiral Cunningham to send us men to man these vessels, of which we had fifteen (?). These were coming from Malta, all disguised as civilian seamen, when the river opened.

The great up-river invasion, with a few boats only just strong enough to keep the water out, and little guns that were capable of very little harm, all arrived at Sulina on the Black Sea in an English cargo ship from Malta. [...]

About a hundred officers and ratings had come, all as bogus civilians, and the gear was labelled 'oil-drilling machinery'. It took a day to move it out of the ship and we got it all into one 500-ton dumb-barge. Then we started up the river. While the gear was being shifted I had time to size up the men. I liked them. They had all volunteered, in Malta, for a 'risky job'. [...] Before we started we got every officer and rating into the saloon of the big tug *Princess Elizabeth* and I explained to them the general scheme as simply as I could. I firmly believed at that time that by doing this absurd raid up the Danube we could bring the war down to Rumania and that our 'other half' could then destroy the Germans' main oil supply. I believed that this would reduce the German fighting power by at least a year. [...] I believed this so intensely that I made them believe it too [...]

Anyway, the main thing we had to do first was to get all the war-gear out of the dumb-barge into the vessels where it belonged. Sulina had been too full of snoopers. We decided to go on to Giurgiu, where the railway comes southward from Buchurest to the river. We needed cranes and would get them there. So we went on.

As soon as we got to Giurgiu the whole convoy was arrested by the Rumanian Port Authorities.

Their plan was foiled. Mason says the story gets confused from now on, and so it does. What Max wanted to do now is not clear, though Mason says:

Max was operating very vigorously in Buchurest. He seemed thoroughly cheerful about it all, while I felt depressed and furious that the suicide party had struck a snag. Somehow he managed to persuade the Rumanian Foreign Office that we had brought these men to take our ships out from the Danube. And the armament for defence.

The plan does not look good in retrospect. In his 1971 book *Oil and the Romanian State* the historian Maurice Pearton says, 'The British position was further compromised by an outstandingly maladroit attempt by the British navy to blow up the Iron Gates, at the beginning of Apr. 1940.' This 'maladroit' plan seems to be the same as that described below, which Barker calls the 'Despard plan:'

> The third possibility was to block the Iron Gates by sinking cement-filled barges in the narrows. Section D had originally considered this, as had the French 5th Bureau. But the plan passed into the hands of the Director of Naval Intelligence, Admiral Godfrey, and the naval Attaché in Bucharest and Belgrade, Captain Max Despard R.N., a man of powerful personality with a gift for alarming and upsetting British diplomats.

All they could do now was to try to get the ships out. To do so they had to cooperate with the French, a time-consuming business. Mason's job becomes 'increasingly political, for Max despised the Romanians so much that he didn't like to talk to them.' Max and Mason seem very close to events in Romanian politics, dangerous and urgent now on the very brink of war, but equally confusing. Twenty years earlier Max may have hobnobbed with 'nice chaps' from the Romanian royalty, but keeping track of King Carol was a different matter. He had abdicated because of his Jewish mistress Magda Lupescu, but had now returned to power. He had arrested and supposedly stamped out the Fascist Iron Guard but was now working closely with them.

According to Barker, Sir Reginald Hoare was not the stuffed shirt Mason depicts. She calls him 'pleasantly eccentric, but normally sceptical' and credits him with good sense: 'The Minister, Hoare, was a shrewd observer; he was also remarkably outspoken in telling Rumanians what he thought of them, in a way that sometimes alarmed the Foreign Office; but his charm of manner perhaps softened his words.' Barker further points out that the Foreign Office had been reluctant to instigate sabotage in southeastern Europe, wishing to keep on good terms with officially neutral countries. Furthermore she says the British had done little to keep up trade and commerce. This put British diplomats in an awkward position. From Bucharest Sir Reginald Hoare wrote that 'it would rather stick in my gizzard to do anything really disagreeable to the Rumanians in the matter of oil when she is providing that oil in return for the armaments which we and the French have failed to supply.' It was also left to Hoare to do a lot of explaining and mopping up after the debacle of the 'Despard plan.' Max may have been laughing; the Foreign Office was not. This is how it all ended. There is a sad note in the following day by day account of the Second World War for 10 February 1941:

> London: General Ion Antonescu's decision to allow Romania to be used as a base for a massive German Expeditionary force led today to a diplomatic rupture with Britain. After a half-hour meeting with Antonescu, later described as "extremely painful", the British envoy, Sir Reginald Hoare, returned to the legation to pack his bags.

The Romanians had chosen the wrong side. Max is in an enemy country. Max sends Mason home to London to explain the situation. It is the end of his stay in the Balkans. Max repairs to Belgrade.

Was Max 'M'?

'Will the real James Bond please stand up?' So ran the heading of an INSIGHT article in the *Evening Standard*, after the publication of Merlin Minshall's book *Guilt-Edged* in 1975. There have been many Bond candidates. The burning question, at least for Max's younger descendants, is to what extent can we find Max in the James Bond stories? Was Max 'M'? And if so, who was Bond? INSIGHT supports the view that Minshall was the most likely Bond, as does Foot. I do not. This were many elements in Minshall's favour, such as a heady mixture of murdered German spies and explosives disguised as Mackintosh's toffee de luxe, shipped out in the diplomatic bag. He sailed on the Danube, where he met a beautiful German spy who seduced him and later tried to poison him. Yet, as the *Evening Standard* article points out, 'This stirring account, however, is challenged by his partner in the Danube project, Michael Mason, who gets no mention in Minshall's book.' Minshall was supposed to work with Mason, but annoyed him intensely. This is Mason's account:

> My companion Merlin had his good points and his bad ones. He was good company, talkative and clever. He spoke good French, German and Italian. He was about thirty-four and had been about a bit. Well-made and bodily fit by nature. No notion of discipline but capable of deep attachment. There was a reckless streak in him that was bravado rather than boldness. In hard battle he might have

earned a V.C. or he might have run away. I think he was the child of an unhappy marriage and seemed to have no solid ideals beyond having a good time. However, I found him good company, and really liked him, though I realized I could not trust him far out of my sight. He would suddenly start violent quarrels, quite senselessly, with perfectly harmless people. If we sat down to dinner together, peacefully, in a good-class restaurant, he always had to have a row with the *maître d'hotel* about the dinner or with the wine-steward about the wine. Such a bore! Still a little boy showing off.

Minshall was a buccaneer type and fluent in seven languages, but his habit of getting into senseless quarrels was not only annoying but also dangerous and can hardly have been appreciated by the secret services. Nor is flamboyance a qualification for an undercover agent. Minshall frequently refers to his friend Ian Fleming in *Guilt-Edged*. In the tale of his adventures on the Danube he seems to have handled explosives and run sabotage operations entirely on his own, interrupted only by luscious women and troublesome and boring British authorities. The story he relates in his book is curiously parallel to that of Glen and Max, but he mentions neither of them. No wonder: Max made sure he was sent home after one of his ill-disciplined episodes – 'if necessary in irons.'

In his book *The Life of Ian Fleming* (1993) the biographer Donald McCormick also takes a dim view of Minshall and we hear more about the oil sabotage. Max is not mentioned – he has managed to keep in the background:

In these early months of the war Fleming was at times irked by the fact that his was mainly a desk job and he became more and more determined to associate himself with some direct action against the enemy. In the early winter of 1939–40 he was a prime instigator in a plan to try to block the Danube to German ships. Diligent and enthusiastic pressure on his part persuaded Admiral Godfrey to support the initiation of a number of clandestine operations aimed at not only blocking the Danube but crippling the Romanian oil refineries and briefing double agents to take part in these schemes. The project, which involved a small team of officers temporarily attached to the NID, was named Operation Danube. [...]

Officially details of the project have never been admitted, though doubtless they are tucked away in certain secret files. It has been reported that many signals and records of naval affairs were destroyed shortly after the end of the war. Surprisingly, it has been admitted that 'some duplicates can be found in the National Archives in Washington, but may be still classified if the British say so.'

Fleming chose for this operation three men of widely different talents. Appointed as Assistant Naval Attaché, Belgrade, was Alexander Glen, a young RNVR officer educated at Fettes and Balliol College, Oxford, who had been leader of three Oxford University Arctic expeditions between 1932 and 1936. Secondly, and the senior member of the team in age, there was Lt-Commander Michael Mason, a first-class shot and amateur boxer of some distinction, who after Eton and Sandhurst, found himself in the Second World War in the Navy, not the Army. He was sufficiently adaptable to fill all kinds of roles from intelligence operative to commander of a landing-craft flotilla. [...]

The third choice was perhaps the least satisfactory, though justifiable on the grounds of previous service and experience. He was Lt-Commander Merlin Minshall, yet another RNVR officer. Like Mason, he was a first-class shot. A racing motorist before the war, he had also been a karate expert and had been mixed up in some daring escapades among Nazi agents. Some of his enemies dubbed Merlin Minshall 'a bloody pirate,' and he loved to play the role of the secret agent of fiction, a role that became somewhat of a fixation for him as time went on. Indeed, later in life he claimed without justification that Fleming had based the character of James Bond on him. In newspaper and radio interviews in February 1977, Minshall said of Fleming: 'He was ruthless, unsure of himself and a romantic. All the qualities that I had, he wished he had. That's why he used me as his model for Bond.'

[…] As far as Operation Danube was concerned, Michael Mason told me that 'Minshall was a disaster throughout. On one occasion in Glen's presence I had to knock him out to save us all from trouble.'

This is how Barker describes the arrival of Mason and Minshall. She says little of Mason, but her research confirms the unsuitability of Minshall for his task:

In December 1939, as a result of a joint report from the British and French 'naval authorities' in Bucharest, asking for 'experienced personnel' from England and possibly also British crews, the D.N.I. sent to Bucharest two R.N.V.R. officers on 'special service,' Lt Michael Henry Mason and Mr H.G. Minshall. Minshall was given as cover the title of Vice-Consul at Galatz, which deeply distressed the Consul-General, Macrae, who disapproved of his carefree unorthodox activities, particularly a clash with the local police, in circumstances which Macrae regarded as somewhat scandalous. More seriously, Macrae brought a charge of lack of discretion and security: 'stories have been broadcast of wholesale British schemes of sabotage against the interest of the government with which we were on friendly terms…The fantastic posturing of some of the young men involved gave every excuse for gossip if not for credence, particularly as some of the wildest versions can be traced to the amateur Guy Fawkes himself...I am aware I am particularly prejudiced in this matter.'

If I have spent time disqualifying Minshall, it is in order to further another candidate. If Minshall was not Bond, who was? And who was 'M'? Glen comments on the question asked in INSIGHT, concluding that both 'M' and Bond are composite figures, and that one of the many possible candidates for 'M' could have been Max. After all, Max always signed his memos with an 'M.' However, it is likely that his superior Admiral Godfrey, head of Naval Intelligence in London, was more of an 'M.' Fleming was personal assistant to Godfrey. The writer may have assembled his characters at random. He said in an interview that he chose the 'flat' name James Bond from the author of a bird book. In Glen's words in his reply in the *Evening Standard*, 1977:

> "Will the real James Bond please stand up?" asks Insight last week. Rather difficult, I believe, because in the composite picture of James Bond quite a number of people have their part. [....] I did see a good deal of the events of 1939–40 surrounding the plan to make the Danube impassable to German ships – events which Insight described so vividly.
>
> Certainly the Admiralty recognised the importance of the Danube very early indeed, not only in itself but in connection with the Rumanian oil wells, both so vital to the German economy. And Captain Max Despard, whose assistant I was, played a vital part in planning both operations.
>
> "M" certainly has part of Despard in him, rightly, although the

other part is more Admiral John Godfrey, the Director of Intelligence at the Admiralty and one of the most brilliant intelligence officers of his time.

As for the Bond figure, Fleming was not only a friend of Minshall, but also of the man who worked for my father, but did things in his own way, my godfather, the legendary Michael Mason, adventurer, landowner and so much more. Mason may well have been a ruthless thug when needed, but to me he was my cherished godfather 'David.' He gave me *Old Peter's Russian Tales* which instilled in me a love of the Russian people: the children sleeping on the stove; black bread and tea from the samovar; the dreadful witch Baba Yaga with her bony legs and her hut on hen's feet; and far away the protector, the Little Father, the Tsar. 'Mr Cucumber,' the knitted toy monkey Mason gave me, he was said to have knitted himself.

Mason fits the Bond stereotype in many ways. He mainly worked on his own and he was capable of astounding acts of bravery and unpleasantness: *Fortiter in re, suaviter in modo,* charm and fists. He was a great linguist and good company when he chose to be; he knew how to wear a dinner jacket, but despised many of the other people who did. He loathed puffed-up bureaucrats and whoever fell into the category of 'pansies.' Those who worked for the British Council were not his type. Neither he nor Max could be described as 'aesthetes' and they had little time for the British Council's 'civilizing mission.' Political correctness, as we know it, was not a requisite for the armed services:

The Germans were not the only people to hate me. One night Max and I were dining at the Capsa, by far the best restaurant in Bucharest. I suddenly saw his face stiffen in horror at something behind me, turned round and saw half a dozen young English creatures dressed as men, who had just come in, all standing and kissing each other across a table.

'Good God Almighty!' said Max.

'I think they are British Council: spreaders of culture among the unenlightened. [...] What shall I do to them, Skipper?'

'Boot the little bastards out of the country! Good God! Do you see those Germans laughing?' I had seen them. About five of Audrey's Gestapo, laughing their heads off.

[...] All were aged between twenty-one and twenty-eight! In time of war! Apparently their job was to teach Rumanian prostitutes to speak good English to enlarge their *clientéle*.

A most Bond-like episode is related by Mason. It concerns one of Lady Hoare's last receptions, 'still full fig, decorations and tiaras.' The 'absurd old man' is what Mason calls 'His Britannic Majesty's etc. etc.,' i.e. the Minister, Sir Reginald Hoare:

I suppose this absurd old man had noticed I talked the King's English so to my horror I found myself invited to an afternoon party at the Ministry. I had meant to avoid anything like that. I was a Vice-Consul – the scum of the earth – less than dust. I wanted to keep among the scum when outside Max's office.

I want to this damned party thinking only of how to get away. It was done for me, beautifully and by chance, by Blackley. A servant called me to the telephone before I'd been in the place ten minutes.

'Look here, Davie!! I'm in the hell of a bloody mess! I've just strangled a woman in the snow!'

'Why in the snow?'

'Christ, man! The snow's everywhere!'

'Is she dead?'

'No. She was picking my pocket! She was working for the Germans! It's the first time I've ever handled a woman with violence....'

I went straight to my hostess, with a joyous song in my heart.

'Lady Hoare, I'm terribly sorry, but I'm afraid I must say goodbye. And with it, my heartfelt thanks. A subordinate of mine has just strangled a woman in the snow. I must go and see if she is dead, and, if so, why. Terribly sad to rush off like this.'

Naturally I was never asked again.

The woman was some barmaid of Blackley's.

The plot thickens. Almost as a postscript Mason describes an extraordinary operation. They needed top-trained Commandos, and Max knew where to find them:

Max had arranged with one of the very top people in Israel for more than fifteen thousand Polish Jews to escape through Rumania to the free countries of the Mediterranean. I had some part in this but much had been done before I got there. As soon as the river opened I ferried a good number across to Yugo-Slavia complete with false passports. Poles are very clever at forgery. There may have been many more than 15,000. Max's price was 300 Israelite gun-men, highly trained, to send wherever they were needed. Three minutes settled the deal. Max said that man had the best brain he ever encountered, and was the easiest to deal with.

The full horrors of the Nazi regime were not yet known and it was not unusual in those days for British to adopt an anti-Semitic tone. Yet this manner of speaking did not always prevent sympathy for persecuted Jews or efforts to help them. But how was such a large-scale operation possible? One reason may perhaps be found in Giles Mac-Donogh's book *1938: Hitler's Gamble* (2009). MacDonogh says that as it was in Hitler's interests to get rid of Jews he actually turned them into a financial transaction. He needed foreign currency. Visas were sold to Jews who surrendered their assets to the Nazis. All over Europe embassies, consulates and chaplaincies were being besieged by Jews. There were mass conversions by Anglican clergy willing to help. It is not clear to what extent the Hagana, the Zionist military organization, was involved. At this point British authorities did not officially recognize the organization, yet it seems they did have common interests and did work together. Max was not alone in helping Jews, but what happened to all these people? I knew my father had helped some Jews, but I thought it was a few people or a family. Fifteen thousand? Some must have survived even after the Mediterranean countries were occupied.

Is this the same plan as the following one described by Barker?

A totally different plan for destroying the Rumanians oilfields quite independently of the Rumanians was considered by the British shortly before the war started, but was nipped in the bud. The Jewish leader, Chaim Weizmann, offered the services of the Jewish Agency to the British through Sir Robert Vansittart, then Diplomatic Adviser to the Foreign Office, who charged Section D with maintaining contact with the Jewish Agency. Simultaneously a Jewish Agency representative in Bucharest approached the British Legation, offering the use of the system of underground escape routes for Jews from Rumania. The consequence was a meeting in the Waldorf Hotel in London between Section D's representatives, including George Taylor, and Jewish Agency representatives including David Ben Gurion and Moshe Shertok (later Sharett) who put forward a plan for an attack on the oilfields by picked men from the inner core of the Jewish Hagana, who would make their own escape from Rumania afterwards. […] The Foreign Office strongly opposed any such undertaking in a neutral country. The scheme died.

If Max was 'M' or partially 'M,' we shall never know. Such is the nature of a diplomat's work: to set up connections, to remain rather loftily in the background. If discretion and delicacy are requisite for peacetime diplomats, then secrecy is essential for a diplomat at war. Much of Max's work was to take decisions that were not put on record, to approve of or wink at actions which he could not condone publicly. He was closely linked to Naval Intelligence in London, but as a senior diplomat he could not become involved in cloak-and-dagger business. At least officially. His job in the Balkans may have turned out to be more exciting than he had anticipated. It was also to prove his mettle. The *Broke* had given him a good start in his career, but he was fortunate then to be in the right place at the right time and under a most able superior. Now twenty years later, and after he had worked as a diplomat for a decade, he was to exercise his qualities of leadership in dramatic circumstances. After the heady events of the last war he had been involuntarily retired from active service and had to live according to protocol. Now there was urgency, a foul enemy, and need for action. The question is whether at times he felt he was back on the *Broke*. I also wonder whether he asked himself what Evans would have done. Evans was impulsive and an enthusiast, but Evans assessed the strength of his enemy.

It was rather a shock for me to find the following comment on my father tucked away in Barker's account. 'The Foreign Office commented: "he is a man who is always liable to let his somewhat wild enthusiasm run away with him…but he is unfortunately the apple of the Admiralty's eye". Despard then made Belgrade his headquarters.' It is disconcertingly double-edged, a troubling hint as to Max's status in the Legation and one explanation of his departure from Romania. He is a mote in the eye of the Foreign Office, but the apple of the Admiralty's eye. He was the Admiralty's man; the Admiralty had originally sent him to the Balkans, and Naval Intelligence had given him 'wide duties,' encouraging him to encourage others in activities that would trouble the Legation. We saw in his letter from his first stay in Romania that he was troubled by what he saw as diplomatic narrow-mindedness. Max was a doer. This does not mean that he did not think. It may mean that he did not reflect enough or take heed of the counsel of others. Glen implies that Max did not understand the new type of warfare, that his political judgement was not adequate. Glen may have been right. Was the tugboat action simply a foolhardy gesture? Mason calls it a suicide plan, and indeed the loss of life would have been horrific. At first I thought Glen was wrong when he hinted at Max's lack of political acumen, describing him as 'totally unreal' in his assessment of the enemy strength. I thought it might have been Max's way of keeping up spirits, both of himself and others. Now I think that Glen was perhaps being guarded in his assessment of what must have been a brave but essentially ill-conceived plan. It was dependent on the reaction of greater powers. Did the British actually think Romania would be on the allied side? In her *Balkan Trilogy* Manning rather cruelly parodied a British attack on Ploesti, but the plans cannot have been as half-baked or as widely publicized as the plan she parodied. Nor did Max act entirely on his own; the plan was approved of by Section D.

Yugoslavia

As to Yugoslavia, ancient geographic, ethnic and religious differences were very much alive under the blanket of unity. Among the Serbs there was a strong anti-German sentiment, favourable to Britain. And the Serbs were very different from the Romanians, according to Glen. Glen was very much in favour of the Serbs, having met and fallen in love with Zorica, who was to remain his wife for the rest of his life. He outlines the delicate territory in which Max was now to use his skills:

> British policy in Yugoslavia in 1940 was very clear: to help and maintain Yugoslav neutrality and to encourage Yugoslavia against sliding into any association with the Axis powers. Yet at the same time, Britain was undertaking covert operations against the Axis on Yugoslav territory. A careful and difficult balance was required, lest those activities called down Axis reaction which could be irresistible.

Glen records that 'I feel fortunate in having been involved in the partially abortive sabotage activities in Romania and Yugoslavia in 1940/41.' Like Mason, he was recruited by Naval Intelligence in December 1939:

> I was summoned by the Director of Naval Intelligence (DNI) Admiral

John Godfrey. His orders were simple: 'Cause havoc on the Danube by any means.'

But this first interview with the DNI did not start on a particularly promising note.

'I'm sending you to Belgrade as assistant to Captain Despard, the Naval Attaché there,' said the Admiral.

'Thank you, sir,' I stuttered, racking my brains for some recognition of Balkans territory. 'I'm very interested in …mmm… Romania, sir.'

'Well, that ought to stand you in good stead in Yugoslavia,' said the Admiral, displaying the slightest suspicion of a smile. 'Captain Despard is Naval Attaché with rather wide duties. Spend a few days in the Section and find out which country is which. The Danube is our interest and both countries may be key.'

In Belgrade Glen met Max, and this is where the narratives of Glen and Mason overlap a good deal. This is partly because Glen quotes Mason lavishly. Glen published his book at a ripe old age in 2002 when Mason had been dead for many years. However, Mason's book of 1966 was still not public property. Mason covers the first period in Romania, while Glen is sent to Belgrade. Glen's *Target Danube* provides a thorough firsthand account and analysis of this period in Yugoslavia. Glen on the whole writes well of all the Allies, saving his invective for the enemy. It is a pleasure to note his praise of Max, as in this recollection of their first encounter:

It was against this background that I joined forces with the formidable and colourful Captain Max Despard DSC, RN, the British Naval Attaché to Belgrade and Bucharest. I was to discover Despard had his fingers in many pies […]

The impact of Max Despard was dramatic! He was huge, with a massive head, dominant in every way, incisive and cutting. Anglo-Irish in family, his brilliant First World War career was terminated by a delayed explosion of a 4.7 inch shell which took away part of his hip, but only after he had won his Distinguished Service Cross as First Lieutenant on HMS *Broke*, in Captain E.R.G. Evans' epic attack on seven German destroyers.

Despard could relax and enjoy; alternatively he could withdraw into himself. He was in constant pain but rarely showed it. Some of his views were totally unreal, such as that we had no need of any outside help to defeat Germany. But when the going for Britain turned bad, as it did in the Spring of 1940, his courage stood out like a beacon.

Much work was done with Max in his 'comfortable villa at Dedigne.' Dedigne is still a fashionable suburb of Belgrade; it was the home of diplomats and the Yugoslavian upper class. These were later thrown out and replaced by Communist officials. In our time people like Slobodan Milosovic and the notorious criminal Arkhan have lived there. Max appears to be on his way out, according to Glen:

Autumn came and the effects of the long summer heat of 1940 on Max Despard's old wounds were all too obvious. His pain was excruciating and stoical as he was, a limit had been reached.

His was a serious loss. Few matched his understanding of the complexity of our friends, devious and cunning, coupled with utter loyalty for a past which could be more compelling than the present.

Glen seems to be writing Max out of the picture. Is he glossing over the fact that the Foreign Office was exasperated by Max? I feel that he considers Max out of his depth in macro-politics and somewhat impetuous in his need for action. The Danube chapter marks the peak of Max's career and yet there is so much that is uncertain. It is not easy to find out what happened seventy years ago. It was a hectic time and they were all bound by secrecy. Mason's and Glen's accounts were written respectively fifteen and sixty years after the events. Glen lets Max fade out of his narrative in late autumn, but according to Barker he was active as a diplomat in secret negotiations with the Serbian Peasant Party. The British pinned their hopes on this party – 'this down-to-earth solid lot,' according to Glen.

Max was certainly very much present in Belgrade when the city was bombed on 6 April 1941. My father left Belgrade in a dramatic manner. On 25 March the Prime Minister Cvetkovic and Foreign Minister Cincar-Markovic had signed a working agreement in Berlin with Germany and Italy. The next day the daily paper *Politika* published the full text of the agreement. This was not well received in Belgrade. There were massive protests on 27 March: '*Bolje Pakt, nego Rat*' and '*Bolje grob nego rob*' – 'Better the grave than a slave' – chanted the people of Belgrade, who had risen as one. The government was overthrown in an anti-German coup and the young Petar was sworn in as king of Yugoslavia. Churchill declared that 'Yugoslavia has found its soul.' But the German response to the Yugoslavian uprising was savage. Hitler was preparing for Operation Barbarossa into Russia, scheduled for June 1941. Any deflection of troops and energy caused mighty irritation. In Operation Punishment (German: *Fall Bestrafung*) there was no mercy for *Untermensch* Slavs.

Early in the morning on 6 April 1941, the Germans bombed the city. The Germans and their allies invaded speedily and Yugoslavia fell apart like a stack of cards.

I'm not sure we can always judge Max by what he did – there is so much we cannot know – but we do have an idea of the manner in which he did it. And certainly Max proved his qualities of leadership in the last part of his Balkan period. He showed the force of his personality and his ability to act in demanding situations. This was no longer the time for diplomatic protocol; the task that remained was daunting. In the period before the war the edges of diplomacy were blurred. It is normal in almost all countries to conduct some degree of espionage or information gathering. Max was after all closely linked to Naval Intelligence. The tension in legations before the outbreak of hostilities is electric, with conflicting telegrams and rumours and no one quite knowing what is going on. Then comes the declaration of war. There are people clamouring at the gates for protection; the Ambassador may himself be seen in shirtsleeves packing crates, as was the American Ambassador Riddle, according to Maitland; and there is the smell of burning documents. A diplomat in time of war is *persona non grata* and must be expelled, though under the conventions he and his charges must be guaranteed safe conduct. Max's responsibility was now to collect any British citizens and bring them to safety away from what had become enemy territory. Not all were British citizens. We shall see in Maitland's account that diplomatic status was generously conferred.

Recent research has revealed that the Nazis were not squeamish in extending the scope of their diplomatic corps. In 1941 the foreign office in Berlin received a handwritten claim for travelling expenses from Franz Rademacher. Purpose of journey: 'Liquidation of Jews in Belgrade.' In contrast we have Max's own claim for expenses to the Director of Navy Accounts, Admiralty, Bath in 1942. The letter gives a stark account of his convoluted journey from Belgrade:

Travelling Expenses – Captain M.C. Despard, DSC., R.N.

With reference to the attached claim for travelling expenses and subsistence for the period 6th. April, 1941 to 18th. July, 1941, it is requested that the details of sum due may be completed in the Admiralty as the scale of subsistence is not known here.

2.It is remarked that the journey from Belgrade to Kotor was made in my own car as far as Sarajevo, where it was bombed and burnt out; the journey to Kotor was completed in a second car I requisitioned from Belgrade. Further, from Belgrade I first went East and South along the Nis Road as far as Kragigevac and then returned to Zvornic via Belgrade and from Zvornic to Sarajevo and from there to Kotor via Gasko and Trebinje. The total distance must have been about 900 miles.

3.From Kotor on the 2nd. of May, until leaving Chinciano [Chianciano] on the 12th.July, I was fed and accommodated by the Italian Government. The scale of feeding necessitated considerable supplementary purchases, and I consider I should be allowed half subsistence for this period. All purchases of food, petrol, repairs for the journey from Belgrade to Kotor were paid for.

4.Mr. C.E. Everett, my Secretary, now Consular Shipping Advisor at Oporto was with me throughout and it is requested that sum is allowed me may be allowed him on the appropriate scale as a Lieutenant R.N.V.R.

To an outsider this sounds like the synopsis of a Tintin book. It was serious enough – and chaotic. Max had to leave his villa and his possessions in Dedigne. When Belgrade was bombed he packed a couple of suitcases, arranged transport and spent the morning rounding up British residents. His main responsibility was to ensure their safety now that Yugoslavia was occupied. They were permitted one suitcase per person. Not only British residents were his responsibility. Among those fleeing were high-ranking Yugoslavian politicians who needed to escape the Nazis. Diplomatic credentials were liberally bestowed.

Seven cars and a lorry set off in convoy going south and west over the high passes in the Bosnian mountains. They lost two vehicles in a snowdrift. The aim was to reach Greece and the Middle East. However, it became impossible to go to Greece. The odyssey out of Yugoslavia is described by Maitland in my father's obituary and in more detail in his book *European Dateline* from 1946. Maitland was *The Times* correspondent. He knew the Balkans well; he was well versed in the intricacies of Balkan politics and had followed the advance of the occupying powers from country to country. When Belgrade was so devastatingly bombed on 6 April he was mainly concerned with getting his story out. He had a car and drove out of the city, heading for the Greek border. Next morning he arrived at Vrnjacka Banja where most of the British colony, the Minister, the Service Attachés and the rest of the Legation found themselves. This is where Max comes into his own; he is in charge and takes care to avoid red tape. Maitland met Max:

> The character who from now on stood out was Captain Despard, the British Naval Attaché, known as "The Skipper". ..a gigantic Irishman …He has a sense of humour and much humility. He is tall, heavy, never pretends to be a hero, will admit as readily as any man that he knows what it is to be frightened. His readiness to do a job of work and his humour and decision bucked us all up.

They now heard that Skopje had fallen: 'So far as Greece is concerned, we're done for. We'll now have to make for the coast.' So they had to change their route:

The only hope of getting out was through rocky, snowy Bosnia down to the Dalmatian coast and hope to escape with our stories by sea.

The day before this everybody in the British party had looked indescribably grubby. Now we braced ourselves. We shaved. Those who had clean collars put them on. We straightened out crumpled shirts, adjusted our cuffs, washed handkerchiefs, socks, pared our nails, generally brushed up. If we were to meet the enemy, let's face him clean. [....] I made the rash decision to abandon journalism till we got out, and meanwhile lend a hand to help the party as a whole. [....] I offered my services to the Skipper in any capacity in which I might be useful. He took me on his staff as chauffeur and interpreter. [Maitland's wife was Serbian][....] the Skipper had to get to Zvornik in Bosnia, where the General Staff was installed, to make contact with the Yugoslav Navy. Hugh MacDonald had also to go there to meet the Yugoslav Air Staff.

Maitland had now laid aside his role as journalist. His son Ian tells me that my father wrote out Maitland's credentials as a diplomat on a piece of toilet paper. Such were the times. Their aim was Zvornik, 'a kind of Christmas-card fairyland.' In 'deep caverns burrowed into the mountain heart' was the General Staff. After eggs and bacon and *rakija* they set off next day on steep icy mountain roads to Sarajevo. There they once more were bombed, now specially targeted as the Germans were following the route of the Diplomatic Corps. The diplomats were to be installed at Ilidja, a mountain village. There they were joined by Charles Everett, Lieutenant of the Royal Naval Volunteer Reserve, Max's assistant, mentioned in Max's claims for expenses. So now they were four. Both Sarajevo and Ilidja were soon heavily bombed, as their hide-out had been spotted by the enemy. After concealing the car as best they could, they ducked. 'At the roadside Charles and the Skipper and I buried our noses in rabbit holes, learned a great deal of botany, and hoped the enemy would ignore our posteriors.'

Communications had broken down, but not all journalists did as Maitland did. Leigh White in his somewhat sensational book of 1944, *The Long Balkan Night*, relates how he threw in his lot with some other journalists who would stop at nothing to get their copy through. There was one portable radio which 'belonged to the British Legation, and was operated jointly by the British military and naval attachés, Colonel Clarke and Captain Maximilian Despard.' The journalists were extremely annoyed with the officers, who would not allow the radio to be used for anything but strictly military purposes. White's book was largely ignored until the 1990s Balkan wars, when it became cult reading.

Max and his party then drove through Dalmatia, country so beautiful that they even stopped to admire the view. And 'at last, joy of joys, we saw the sea. And a ship. It spelt life, safety…' They had arrived at Kotor. They found a house, slept heavily and looked forward to the arrival of 'two seaplanes [that] were coming to take off the forty of our party [Yugoslavian politicians] who would be in the greatest danger if we were caught.' I do not know who these politicians were or what became of them. Maitland wrote up the despatch he hoped to send from Athens. But this was not to be. 'The Skipper' announced that the Yugoslav General Staff, unknown to the British Military Liaison staff, had been engaged in secret armistice parleys. It was the end.

Kotor is a picturesque medieval city with a spectacularly lovely bay. However, Max and his party had other concerns. The population of Kotor was mainly Croat and now turned against the British. Max and Maitland tried to find a boat in order to escape. There was a message from Athens that a destroyer would await them off Kotor bay and rescue them. They got hold of two boats and waited through the night outside Kotor. There was no destroyer. On their return to the harbour they were met by the sight of Italian 'motor-cyclists with machine guns mounted on their handlebars.' They were now prisoners. Italian soldiers had taken Kotor, and

> more or less obnoxious and roving bands of undisciplined, bombastic little men burst in, brandishing a whip on one occasion, for ever demanding food and drink. The only man on our side who did anything to curb these inroads was Despard. At intervals he put on his uniform and with a wave of his robust arm – he is a towering person – dispersed the unruly visitors. Our life soon settled down and though invasions were not stopped altogether, we soon struck up reasonably friendly relations with the sentries. Eighteen out of twenty-one of them said they believed in a British victory.

I have been to Kotor. It is indeed beautiful with a city wall steeply climbing the hill to lookout turrets. I went there hoping to find out more about Max's capture, but I became even more confused. I cannot understand where the destroyer was to meet him and Maitland. There is an isthmus not too far from Kotor, but the bay of Kotor, essentially a fiord, is large and stretches right out to the open sea not far from Herceg Novi. However, seeing the steep mountains round Kotor I did get some idea of their intrepid journey to get there. The prisoners must have been taken away either by ship or by the coastal road that goes north to Dalmatia. Maitland is vague on this point, but his son tells me that in Italy they were interned mainly in Chianciano, probably in the ancient fort.

Altogether they were interned by the Italians for two months. 'I was fed and accommodated by the Italian government,' writes Max.

They were hungry at times, yet did not suffer greatly, although the Gestapo would have liked to treat them more harshly. Most of the Italians hated the Germans. The question was whether the whole party could expect the treatment due to officers and members of the Legation. As Maitland said, 'Though some of us had pretty phoney credentials, it was a kind of return gesture for the excellent and generous British treatment of Italian prisoners in Africa.' While waiting for deliberations over their fate at a higher level they were 'allowed two hours' exercise morning and afternoon and up to twenty of us could go on country walks attended by detectives in lounge suits, Homburg hats, and adorned with umbrellas.'

Their release was in exchange for prisoners from the other side. According to Foot

> the Belgrade legation had to be hurriedly closed down, leaving the mission to pick its way out if it could. The legation staff in Italy had trouble enough in getting away; they were held for several weeks while the status of some of their more dubious members was disputed and were exchanged eventually for the staff of the Duke of Aosta, who had become prisoners at the end of the campaign he lost in Abyssinia.

Their safety depended on the Foreign Office making sure that they could pass through France without being 'molested' by the Germans. In the end a guarantee from Vichy France was secured and after some negotiating Spanish and Portuguese transit visas were obtained. The British boarded a special sealed train. There were fond farewells from the villagers who had sold a lot of beer to them. 'Our detectives were merry too; we had taught them some English songs, and these we all sang together on the station at Mentone.'

After a 'dull' journey through France, they arrived at Lisbon on 17 June 1941. When Herbert and Anita met Max at Euston they thought he was very fat.

Max had had a dramatic journey. He had proved himself a leader of men, managing to extricate so many British citizens as well as Yugoslavians in danger. There had been light-hearted moments and he returned unscathed. However, realities had now moved beyond the sphere of James Bond. Max did not forget those he left behind. He is staunchly on the side of the Serbs, and on his return to England he made a full report on the atrocities being committed in Yugoslavia:

> ...Throughout CROATIA a systematic massacre of Serbs was carried out, the victims numbering "several tens of thousands" and in some towns, such as BANJALUKA in BOSNIA, the entire Serb population has been wiped out.
>
> ...When RUSSIA was attacked by GERMANY, the Communists opened up serious guerilla warfare against the Axis forces in YUGOSLAVIA, and by acting independently, and by bad strategy, much suffering was caused to many innocent Serbs.
>
> Among these "partisans" or "peasant guerilla fighters" who comprise Serbs, Bosnians, Slovenes and Croats, are to be found "left wingers" in various shades of rosy pink to red whose ideological, anti-Fascist, Communist or Russophile views run a very close second to their Nationalist views.
>
> Conditions amounting virtually to civil war have existed between Mihailovitch's CHETNIKS of the right and these leftist partisans, involving, it is alleged, co-operation with the forces of Neditch the Quisling Serbian Premier.
>
> In the face of the ferocious reprisals by the Axis forces, such as

the slaughter of 2,300 civilians, including boys of 16 and 17, by the Germans at KRAGUJEVAC last November, as reprisal for the killing of 26 German soldiers, or the shooting of 200 people in ZAGREB in connection with the killing of three German officers, Mihailovitch advocated the temporary suspension of operations and concentration on preparations for a rising at a more favourable moment.

This would seem to explain the criticism of his collusion with the Axis and the criticism that all the fighting was now being done by partisans.

Max's conclusion is clear and his appeal is to London:

... Serbia is living through the greatest tragedy of her history; chaos, internecine strife and misery are her lot to-day – even greater, much greater, than in the last war of 1914-18.

*Max (second from right) talking to King Haakon VII of Norway.
To the left is the Mayor of Cardiff (1942–4).*

Cardiff

When he returned, Max had private affairs to sort out, such as trying to obtain compensation for the loss of property when he left his house and possessions in Belgrade. In 1942 he was trying to get in touch with fellow cadets from Dartmouth in 1905. Almost half of them were dead.

He worked for a while at the Admiralty, from six in the morning until all hours, according to Lilanna in a letter to her mother. I have before me a report, *THE DANUBE (M10 1942)*, compiled by the War Office in July 1942. It is Copy No.14, marked SECRET, and it contains detailed photographs of the river, plus detailed statistics on shipping tonnage and towing power and 'Estimated German Imports 1942,' whereof cereals are by far the largest item. There are also chapters devoted to 'Vulnerable points on the Danube.' The War Office states that 'This report has been prepared in collaboration with the Chief of the Technical and Navigation Sections of the International Danube Commission from its inception in 1920 till 1939, and most of the statistical data embodied are from the official records of the Commission.' Did Max have a hand in this?

I hope he had the opportunity to state his views on Serbia during the debriefing. He was also being prepared for his next job. He was posted to Cardiff as Chief of Staff, Western Approaches. The Flag Officer-in-Charge was Admiral Sir Rudolph M. Burmester, RN (retired).

This may have seemed like a dull routine job compared with

the excitements of the Danube and all the opportunities he had had for taking initiatives. And yet this was probably his most important job. Operation Neptune was the code-name for the landings phase of Operation Overlord, the planned invasion of France – D-Day. It was shrouded in secrecy. In an interview with the BBC in 2003, Burmester's personal secretary relates how she 'worked in a basement with whitewashed windows and a typewriter which was locked up every night. All carbons were burnt as a security measure, and I did not mix with others in the canteen…Documents were marked "Too secret" rather than "Top secret".'

As Chief of Staff for the Bristol Channel area Max was responsible for liaising with the first American unit for the Normandy invasion. While he was there the build-up of American forces in Britain was in full swing and the Cardiff area was one of the places where they were landing. Max's job was to see that this was well carried out. This entailed getting the Americans ashore and then getting them off again to their camps, dealing with mines laid by enemy aircraft, finding docks, finding escorts, landing thousands of tanks, trucks, jeeps, artillery, 'ducks' (floating trucks) and any number of men. Herbert remembers him entertaining senior American counterparts, and he also remembers him continually being called out at night to deal with emergencies. Towards the end of the war, in a letter dated 17 February 1945, the Admiralty thanked my father for his 'good services in the planning and execution of the operations for the invasion of Normandy.' He was but a cog in the wheel, but it was a wheel that rolled over the Channel and put an end to Nazi rule in Europe. I imagine many such letters were sent out, but it is gratifying to know that his was no small contribution.

He remained in Cardiff until the end of the war. Some of the time the family joined him there. There was at one point a 'dreadful'

WRENs lined up for Annabelle's christening, Cardiff, 11 September 1943.

flat overrun with mice, even with a dead mouse in the fridge. Anita remembers a smallish house at Penarth which Lilanna very much liked as it was small and warm. Colbury was kept on and they went back for the holidays. There were no long summer holidays in Ula in wartime. Anita and Herbert were away at school and did well. Max encouraged the education of his children and Lilanna followed up. Max was not a lover of the arts. When Lilanna later saw a school play with one of the children, she admitted that the production was good, but she wrote to her mother that she did not think the school should be spending time and effort on such things. As a theatre lover I find this attitude unpleasantly utilitarian and surprising; where was that small library of French poetry? Is she just echoing Max or is it part of her Norwegian Lutheran education? Ibsen's works were read as literature in Norway, but there was not much room for play-acting. My mother also seems to have missed the point that working together in a school play had a larger social purpose as well as the aesthetic. But then neither Max nor any of his children enjoyed team games. Max's books all disappeared so I do not know what he read. Terence liked blood and action, such as Icelandic sagas and Wilbur Smith thrillers.

While in Cardiff Max and Lilanna had a new baby. The Allies landed in Sicily on 10 July 1943, the day I was born. It was the day before my mother's fortieth birthday. My father was fifty-one. At the christening on 11 September Wrens were lined up along the street. The beginning of my story is near the end of my father's. From now on the story is also mine, as it is partly based on my own memories. A child celebrates its birthday, but not its conception. No one likes to think of their parents involved in the activities that result in a child. Yet I like to think that my parents loved each other deeply and that they were happy to be together after years of war, uncertainty and much separation.

Terence was at sea during the war. To start with he was on the lower deck of a destroyer, HMS *Boreas,* based in Freetown, Sierra Leone to cover the South Atlantic. He worked through the system; he started the war as an ordinary seaman on a destroyer and sailed two years escorting ships on their journey to the Cape to supply Egypt, to avoid the Mediterranean. He had a hard time, below decks, sharing a minimum of space with a rough crowd. He had terrible memories of Freetown: the heat, the humidity, sharks off the beach, mosquitoes and malaria. These were hard years, with the danger, the enemy without and the tough company within in a tense, cramped space under decks. He was later commissioned and as a Lieutenant became

Lilanna and Annabelle in Cardiff, 1946.

the anti-submarine officer on HMS *Tintagel Castle*, a frigate in the North Atlantic, which succeeded in sinking a U-boat. He led the hunt and fired a torpedo, as his father had done, and he was extremely proud of the part he played in this action.

All was not hardship and battle. Terence could relate stories of poetic quality, of stars at night and St Elmo's fire playing in the rigging and on the masts after a storm. At one point HMS *Boreas* was ordered to travel at full speed. They sailed for twenty-four hours with the funnel glowing. Then at night they arrived at an extraordinary scene, at what looked like a village or city full of lights. A troop ship, the *Empress of Canada*, carrying 1,800 men, had been sunk and these were the lights on the lifebelts of the survivors. Terence's destroyer alone took on board 811 of them. The ship was now so overloaded that she had to go at minimum speed. There were many Italian prisoners. Terence showed such kindness that one of them gave him a handmade aluminium ring, a memento he very much cared for. There were also ATS (Auxiliary Territorial Service) girls, or as he said 'many of the men,' who were pregnant.

Whereas the first part was spent in the heat of West Africa, the last years took him to the North Atlantic, escorting convoys from Newfoundland, now as an officer. He vividly tells of the time the entire convoy – that is, ninety-seven ships – slowed to a standstill. The instruments had picked up a shadow which they thought was a U-boat, but which turned out to be a giant iceberg. The whole convoy stood still while the monster sailed through at a speed of 5–7 knots.

He had served in the South Atlantic, the North Atlantic and the Mediterranean at the time of the Operation Torch landings, the British-American invasion of French North Africa. He now sought a change from seagoing and took a course in marine diving and explosives – something he said every young man should have experience of. There he joined John Edmonds in salvage, clearing the Thames estuary of wrecks. This was perhaps the best part of the war for Terence, and John became a lifelong friend of the family. Terence was extremely good with his hands, skilful whether it came to working with dynamite or with fishing-tackle. The war ended on a good note for Terence. He was on one of the first ships to Norway in 1945 when he could use his knowledge of the Norwegian system of buoys and sea marks. He could also return to his beloved Ula. Terence was to end his days in an old people's home near Ula. The war was still

Admiral Sir Rudolf M. Burmester, Flag Officer-in-Charge, Cardiff (1942–3).

with him. Once I gave him a packet of sweets and he tucked them away for spare ammunition.

As for Max, after the war he was, like thousands of other officers, faced with the question of employment. His case was made complicated by the fact that he had originally been invalided out of the Navy and then seconded to the services of the Foreign Office. He risked being passed from one of these bodies to the next. In June 1945 he writes to Burmester, the Flag Officer-in-Charge, Cardiff. Subject: 'Loss of Kit.' He reminds him of the claim sent in earlier when he had lost personal belongings amounting to some £800 in Belgrade. He asks for a further sum for clothing now that he is to be demobilized.

The family had only recently lived elegantly, with a valet and rooms at the Athénée, and an upper-class life at home, but now Lilanna found herself at times without money. Anita remembers that her mother confided in her about these matters and that when Lilanna's friend Else Werring visited London, Lilanna could not afford to go up to see her.

On 12 July Max again writes to the Flag Officer-in-Charge:

> As the Government have guaranteed that employers shall reinstate in their pre-war jobs, or in similar positions, those called up for war service, and as I was before the war Acting Secretary General and Secretary General Designate of the International Danube Commission, the salary of the post being between £2,000 and £2,500 per annum, and also on a recent visit to the Admiralty I was informed that there were available more senior officers than the Admiralty could employ I decided not to volunteer for further service. I am now naturally interested to know how in my case it is proposed to implement the above guarantee.

On receipt of this letter the Flag Officer-in-Charge writes to the Admiralty on 14 July:

> Although the reinstatement of Captain Despard would seem to be the ultimate concern of the Foreign Office, it is presumed that he was nominated by the Admiralty for this pre war employment, and it is felt that Their Lordships may consider that they have a direct interest in the re-establishment of this officer in similar employment, for which I strongly recommend him, on his release from Naval Service, and will accordingly give the matter their support.

The reply which arrived in Cardiff on 17 September from the Admiralty cannot have been satisfactory:

> ...I am to acquaint you that there is at present no International Commission of the Danube, the River having been brought under effective Soviet military control. 2)The whole matter of the International Waterways is, however, at present under discussion.3) The Foreign Office has in the meantime been requested to note that Captain Despard is willing and available to resume his pre-war post or any other similar office in the event of a revival of the Commission, or the setting up of any equivalent organisation.

It was hardly likely that the Danube commission would be revived. The Iron Curtain was firmly in place. Max's grievances were those of many officers after the war, but his case was complicated. It was put before the Admiralty, who agreed that after so many years of service (since 1933) in the rank he was entitled to call himself Captain. But his pension was based on that of a lieutenant commander in 1926 and no notice was taken of the time he had served as a captain. Max was no longer the apple of the Admiralty's eye. In addition to this negligence was the question of inflation, a 1926 pension not being equivalent to one of 1945. He was no longer under the Admiralty, but it is perhaps strange that he did not apply for other jobs. The whole world was waiting to be reorganized and he had knowledge and experience. He was fifty-three years old and cannot have been satisfied with the prospect of doing very little. Maybe he was just tired.

Bartley Manor in the 1960s.

Last Years

Lot 233 29 Nov 1996 Dix Noonan Webb: Medals: Auction Archive. Lieutenant M.C. Despard, Royal Navy, two groups as worn prior to and after WW2: Six D.S.C., G.V.R.; 1914–15 Star Trio, M.I.D., the war medal with 6 clasps, Mediterranean…Hammer Price £180

Lot 1519, 12 Dec 2012 A great War D.S.C. group of eleven awarded to Captain M.C. Despard, Royal Navy, who was decorated for his gallantry as gunnery Officer of H.M.S Broke during her spectacular encounter with enemy destroyers on the night of 20–21 April 1917 – ramming one of her adversaries at 27 knots, the impact hurled the German destroyer practically over on her beam-ends: but retaliatory fire eventually reduced the Broke to a 'smoking shambles,' her decks in places 'literally running in blood'. Hammer Price £4200

So this is where these and the other medals went. No one in the family had been told.

My father's last years were not happy ones. During the war Terence came of age. He had been out at sea in harsh conditions throughout the war; he deserved some recognition. And now, thanks to the inheritance from his mother he could buy a family home. He and Max settled for Bartley Manor, a house with a farm and about a hundred acres. Max knew little about farming, while Terence had worked on a farm before the war. Terence was also practical and good with his hands. He was very good with animals. He became such an expert at delivering lambs that I'm sure he could have replaced any midwife in the area. However, after the gruelling war years he was also keen on enjoying life, riding at home and skiing in Switzerland. He was also strongly tied to Ula where he went every summer.

The plan was that Max and Terence should run the farm together. This arrangement was far from ideal. The house was too big for the farm, the farm too small for the house. It was a farm for a gentleman farmer, one with another income. Terence had money, but Max's income after the war was not what he had hoped for, and certainly not sufficient for the life he had grown used to. He had lost many of his possessions on leaving Belgrade. As he said, 'I had only the uniform I was wearing.' The transition from active service to a retired life can be traumatic for anyone. For an officer to go from a position of high command to being second in command to his own son can hardly have been desirable or wise. Relations between Terence and his father became strained. I can remember endless meals at Bartley when 'Mr Cucumber' and I were allowed to sit under the dining-room table while Terence and Max quarrelled above.

For me as a child Bartley was paradise. The house was a stately Georgian building covered with wisteria whose overpowering scent filled the bedrooms. The garden was filled with azaleas and rhododendrons and there was a huge oak tree with a swing. We have a photograph of my mother on the swing.

There was a large walled garden with apples, pears, quince, vegetables and raspberries. I roamed about eating raw Brussels sprouts as well as kale and the dogs' dried fish. There was a herd of Guernseys called Harebell, Bluebell, Annabelle and the like. There was a terrifying bull and there were pigs for home consumption. There were two

Lilanna and Annabelle at Bartley, 1947.

dogs, Robin and Susie, and I remember three horses: the cart-horse Jolly, the pony Olly and the mare Molly. The riding horses belonged to Terence. I am grateful for being left so much alone when a child; solitude is healthy for children. At least it helps the imagination. I had wonderful games.

I loved Max's study, which had a comfortable smell, a big desk and a large armchair with an antimacassar. I would sit with Max and my favourite book, a book of Scottish tartans. I slept in the school room, so called because my brothers and sisters had had governesses. I never had a governess or an old-fashioned English nanny. I like to think that my mother enjoyed looking after me. I went to school in Lyndhurst with two old ladies, Miss Gale and Miss Gale. Later I went for a short while to Fritham House, run by Sir Anthony Eden's wife. The uniform was in very good taste and we were taught by her daughters, who must have been supremely unqualified. We learnt Greek dancing and were given a thorough grounding in harness and tackle. Our art lessons consisted of colouring bridles, reins and other tackle on the horses drawn by one of the daughters. I was not aware of the social cachet of the school; to me it was bewildering and silly. I did not like being there and learnt nothing.

Herbert and Anita were seldom confided in by their elders. We all grew up with silences and evasions. Family silences, not military secrets. Asking Anita and Herbert about those years has always caused them pain. A friend of mine was thwarted in love. She told me she had locked the door to her heart and thrown away the key. At the time I was impressed by her fortitude and the sense of drama. Now I am doubtful of the soundness of her enterprise. The heart has valves, not locks; blockage means death.

However, in a large house a child is protected from much pain and distress. In 1948 Lilanna became ill. She died on 12 March 1949 of carcinoma of the liver and suprarenal carcinoma. Little was said; nothing to me. I had to find out for myself. The mid-twentieth century lay between the Victorian obsession with mourning and the public intimacy of grief and bereavement now. I have been asked how I reacted. How does a child of five react? Children are told to be happy at Christmas or on their birthdays, whether it suits them or not. Children are not told they can be sad, or how to be so. I was not told that I had reason to be unhappy; there was no procedure for unhappiness. Most of that time is blanked from my memory; I can only remember being unpleasant and unnecessarily naughty. The grown-ups did everything they could to make life normal for me and I was probably the least miserable. Yet that child of five was marked, given a sense of loss

Left: Lilanna on the swing at Bartley, 1948.
Right: Anita with Annabelle on her lap at Bartley, 1949.

and the knowledge that nothing is permanent or can be taken for granted. Also a measure of resilience.

It was always a treat for me when my godfather 'David' – Michael Mason – came to see us. He always brought me presents, like my beloved 'Mr Cucumber.' It makes me happy to read the tribute he gave our mother:

> The war had caught up with Max in Belgrade, as well he knew it would. They made a gradual half-in-half-out sort of progress home through Italy, France and Spain. He was not back by then. Lilanna had been out in Bucharest for about a fortnight just before the ships-raid-up-river jamboree. At her house, Colbury Manor, we got to know each other well, and after the war we all kept in touch; I think, from my point of view, as much for my affection for her as for my devotion to Max.
>
> She told me that I was the first man she had ever known whom Max absolutely trusted [...] But this had the result of a very happy friendship between us, wherein she treated me as something of a combination between family-priest and family-doctor. She was one of the few women one can think of, over thirty, who is 100 per cent *really* nice. When she died in 1949 one of the pure white lights of my life went out.

The death of a mother is a disaster. There is no longer a family; there are various people trying to keep things going. What was to become of us? Anita had graduated, Herbert was still at Oxford and I was five years old. In February 1951 Terence married. His bride, Valborg Gjersøe, was tall and splendid-looking. She had spent time in America and had, I think, rather hazy notions of what living in the country entailed. She made friends, but never quite cracked the codes. She tried to get on with Max, but he was not receptive. Terence naturally wished to make Bartley a home for his own family. In square feet Bartley may have been large enough to house an extended family, but in practice it was not a good idea.

Max was sixty, and after a life of responsibility and influence he had nothing. The strain of the war years must have taken their toll. He must have been in great pain because of his leg, and now he was a widower again after twenty-four years of marriage. He did not get on with his eldest son. Terence never forgave his banishment to school. He always told me that throughout the war his parents never wrote to him. This is surprising. Max was disappointed in him and was not impressed by his choice of wife. Max was bitter, but stayed on; as he said, to keep things going. The situation became intolerable. He wrote to his mother-in-law in Norway of the pain in his leg when he drove the tractor. He said that his worst trouble was nerves. He also said that drink was no problem and that he would not remarry.

His situation was bad. He had no job. Max had had an allowance from Nora's inheritance. On Terence's marriage this allowance ceased and he was given a lump sum of £10,000. This sounds generous, but there were debts to pay. Max was not wanted at Bartley. According to Anita, Terence told him bluntly, 'You'll have to go' – to which he replied, 'But where am I to go?'

The family broke up. Anita, Herbert and I went to Norway. Anita and Herbert stayed for about half a year while I stayed on with my uncle and aunt for another two years. Anita and Herbert went to London to find jobs, but there was no Admiralty to support them. Anita had done very well at school and it was an achievement that at the end of the war she gained a place at St Anne's, one of the few Oxford women's colleges. She thrived at university, because of the work and because of the many young officers given a university place on demobilization.

Studio portraits of Terence (1945), Anita (late 1940s) and Herbert (also late 1940s).

Opposite page:
Anita sailing in Brittany, 1952.

She had been presented at court, had curtseyed to the King and to a large cake at Queen Charlotte's Ball. Now she and Herbert went from hunt balls to nothing. Caste is largely determined by the management of knives and forks and vowels; its upkeep is dependent on cash. There was none. It is surprising that a man who had all his life relied so much on his father should leave his own children to fend for themselves. Max must have overestimated the power of brains and education to overcome obstacles. He had faith that they would fall on their feet, but when Anita applied for jobs she was told, 'Another B.A. who can't type.' However, she did in the end get quite a good job in the Foreign Office.

I stayed on in Norway with Lilanna's brother Hans Jørgen and his wife Tante Lucie, whom we all adored. Her gift was to make each one of us feel important and wanted. These were good years for me. I was also very happy when after two and a half years I moved to Kent to live with Anita, who had married John Fischel in 1952. They had one baby when I came and there were four more in rapid succession. They treated me as a grown-up among the little ones, but gave me everything a child could need. In 1954 Herbert married Minda Irgens. They had two children: Patrick and Camilla. I am happy to say that I count as my best friends my sister, my brother Herbert and my sister-in-law Minda.

Max did remarry. Ann Nixon in the pub was a war widow, not unwilling to find a new husband. In walked the tragic Captain Despard, still handsome. She must have listened to him and sympathized with his plight. She had a daughter Jennifer, one year older than me. Ann did not have the charm or elegance of Lilanna, but she was straightforward and her robust good humour must have been good for Max. My first meeting with her was not encouraging. John and Anita took me and my friend camping in Scotland. We stayed the night with my father and Ann. It was a forbidding stone house.

Outside the house was a stone where it was said that Covenanters had been put to death. I had no idea what Covenanters were, but my friend was keen on Walter Scott (at least the movies) and was terrified. I was more alarmed by Ann who had few teeth and an enormous bosom.

For a while Max had a job as an appeals organizer for the families of servicemen in Lanarkshire and Glasgow. I suspect that Maitland, then MP for Lanark, helped 'the Skipper' to this appointment. I do not know how long the job lasted. Certainly he and Ann did not stay long in Scotland. Their income evaporated in their frequent moves up and down the country between Lanarkshire, Somerset, Moffat and Devon.

My father rather half-heartedly argued for custody of me, but I was better off where I was. He rarely came to London or Kent to see us, but I went to visit him in the holidays. I got on well with Jennifer, but would not have wanted to spend my days with her, her horse and her other passion, Elvis Presley. I was frightened of the horse and I was jealous of the stepsister who knew my father so well. I don't know how enthusiastic Max was about Elvis, but I remember him as good natured. He may have been happy to see that Jennifer and I were friends. I loved seeing Max. We never talked of anything important. He did not volunteer much and I was too young, or too foolish, to ask him. In the letters I have from him in the late 1950s and early 1960s he talks of his garden, but I was not interested in gardens. Max talked of sending bulbs to Anita and he asks about Herbert. They could not afford a car and he usually ended the letter by saying he had to rush to catch the bus to post the letter. The bus passed once a week. They were beset by troubles with their heating. Their last house in Devon was bought for them by Herbert. Herbert also made sure that Ann spent her last years in comfort. After the war Max had a new operation where they discovered bits of uniform embedded in his leg. His wound had to be dressed daily. I cannot remember him complaining and Herbert says he never took painkillers. Nor do I think they drank immoderately. Herbert says Max only drank sociably or as a painkiller.

Only two of his grandchildren met him. Once, Anita's oldest daughter Belinda came with me. She was six and I was sixteen and we enjoyed taking the many trains from Kent to Devon. It was a happy visit. Patrick, Herbert's son, can also remember him as a tall man with a stick. We had a family lunch in a pub once, sad because Max had become so deaf that he could not follow the general conversation. Terence never let his children meet their grandfather, although the girls went to school close by.

I moved to Norway in 1962. Max and I wrote to each other, but did not telephone. I had not known how ill he was when he died on 15 November 1964. He died of heart failure. His heart had long been so weak that he could not undertake more surgery on his leg. He also had diabetes. He must have been ill for some time as we heard that he had had his bed downstairs and Jennifer had single-handedly carried it up before we came. This tells us that Jennifer was strong. I have never, until quite recently, thought enough about the care Ann and Jennifer gave my father in his illness and the loss they suffered. The cremation was on 19 November at 11.40 in the morning in Bournemouth. It was a miserable funeral. The crematorium was like an assembly line with piped music. We had sandwiches and tea afterwards. No one said anything. No one ate anything either. Not even I did, and I was always hungry. We were all moved that Christopher Parnell came, once more strengthening the link between the two families. Max's brother Tommy was there. I had never met him, only heard of his nightmares after being in a Japanese POW camp. He was so like Max that I was shocked. And yet he was unlike him. There was the sadness.

As consolation one of my old teachers said to me that I had little cause to grieve as I hardly knew him. She missed the point. I had only known the old gentleman in tweeds; the more I find out about him the more I regret that I never knew Max in his uniform, tall, full of laughter, decisive. 'Redoubtable' was one word used of him, 'formidable' another. I started this book as a quest for a lost father. Then as I learnt more I became amazed and delighted by the man of action. I have been confused by his actions and saddened by his setbacks. Our stories overlapped at the end, but now I know him as more than a father, as the sum of his achievements and his pain. And I have grown very fond of him. I hope this book has not been a hagiography, but a reinstatement. My wish is that it has restored some of the dignity and stature that he had at the height of his powers. Many of his qualities live on in his children, grandchildren and their children, for whom the book is written. How he would have loved to see them. In them we see his energy and self-confidence; one has a cleft in his chin; some are practical; many are decisive, able to make a decision 'in three minutes.' Others get on well with all sorts of people, as he did. And his laughter lives on.

Postscript

A happy postscript to the story is that Herbert's son Patrick traced and bought back Max's medals in 2012. They are now in his keeping with Max's full dress uniform, which Terence's eldest son Richard found in the stables at Bartley.

References and Further Reading

Barker, Elisabeth, *British Policy in South-East Europe in the Second World War* (Macmillan, London, 1976).

Blacker, William, *Along the Enchanted Way: A Romanian Story* (John Murray, London, 2009).

Conner, Clifford D., *Colonel Despard: The Life and Times of an Anglo-Irish Rebel* (Signpost Biography, Combined Publishing, Pennsylvania, 2000).

Despard, Richard, http://thecloakofsecrecy.com.

Durrell, Lawrence, *Esprit de Corps* (Faber, London, 1957).

Evans, Captain E.R.G.R., *Keeping the Seas* (Frederick Warne, New York, 1920).

Foot, M.R.D., *SOE: An Outline History of the Special Operations Executive 1940–1946* (The Folio Society, London, 2009 [first published 1984]).

Gandy, Ida, *Staying with the Aunts* (Harvill Press, London, 1963).

Glen, Alexander with Bowen, Leighton, *Target Danube: A River Not Quite Too Far* (The Book Guild, Sussex, 2002).

Gram, Andra & Gram, Steffen, *Turen går til Rumænien* (Politikens Forlag, Copenhagen, 1999).

Hazlewood, Nick, *Savage: Survival, Revenge and the Theory of Evolution* (Hodder and Stoughton, London, 2000).

Hochschild, Adam, *To End All Wars* (Macmillan, London, 2011).

Huntford, Roland, *Shackleton* (Abacus, London, 2002 [first published 1997]).

Hurum, Hans Jørgen, *Franske døgn* (Aschehoug, Oslo, 1942).

Hurum, Gerd Vold, *En kvinne ved navn "Truls"* (Vings, Oslo, 2006).

Jay, Mike, *The Unfortunate Colonel Despard: Hero and Traitor in Britain's First War on Terror* (Bantam Press, London, 2004).

Linklater, Andro, *An Unhusbanded Life: Charlotte Despard: Suffragette, Socialist & Sinn Feiner* (Hutchinson, London, 1980).

MacDonogh, Giles, *1938: Hitler's Gamble* (Constable and Robinson, 2009).

Madden, Richard Robert, *The Life and Times of Robert Emmet, Esq* (P.M. Haverty, New York, 1857 [snippet view]).

Magan, William, *An Irish Boyhood* (The Pentland Press, Durham, 1996).

Magan, William, *The Story of Ireland: a History of an Ancient Family and their Country* (Element Books, Shaftesbury, Dorset, 2000 [first published 1983]).

Magris, Claudio, *Danubio* (Garzanti editore, Milan, 1986: first published in the UK, as *Danube*, by the Harvill Press, 1990).

Maitland, Patrick, *European Dateline* (Quality Press, London, 1946).

Manning, Olivia, *The Balkan Trilogy* (New York Review Books, 2009 [first published in 1960 as *The Great Fortune*])

Mason, Michael, *One Man's War* (Privately printed, 1966).

McCormick, Donald, *The Life of Ian Fleming* (Peter Owen, London, 1993).

Minshall, Merlin, *Guilt-Edged* (Bachman and Turner, London, 1975).

Mønnesland, Svein, *Før Jugoslavia og Etter* (Sypress Forlag, Oslo, 2006).

Mountevans, Admiral Lord, *Adventurous Life* (Hutchinson, London, 1946).

Mulvihill, Margaret, *Charlotte Despard: A Biography* (Pandora, London, 1989).

Oman, Sir Charles, *The Unfortunate Colonel Despard and Other Studies* (Edward Arnold, London, 1922).

Opsahl, Erik (Ed.), *Arne Ordings Dagbøker* (Tano Aschehoug, Oslo, 2000).

Palmer, R.R., *A History of the Modern World* (Alfred A. Knopf, New York, 1964).

Pearton, Maurice, *Oil and the Romanian State* (Clarendon, Oxford, 1971).

Picken, Stuart, *Historical Dictionary of Calvinism* (Scarecrow Press, 2011).

Pocock, Tom, *The Young Nelson in the Americas* (Collins, London, 1980).

Pocock, Tom, *Horatio Nelson* (The Bodley Head, London, 1987).

Pound, Reginald, *Evans of the Broke* (Oxford University Press, 1963).

Public Characters of 1801-1802 (Volume 4), Author Unknown (Printed for Richard Phillips, London, 1801).

Repstad, Pål, *Mannen som ville åpne kirken: Kristian Schjelderups liv* (Universitetsforlaget, Oslo, 1989).

Seim, Jardar, Øst-Europas historie (Aschehoug, Oslo, 1994).

'Taffrail' (Henry Taprell Dorling), *Endless Story* (Hodder and Stoughton, London, 1931).

Thompson, E.P., *The Making of the English Working Class* (Penguin, 1980 [first published 1963]).

Thorkildsen, Dag, *Johannes Ording. Religionsfilosof og apologet* (Universitetsforlaget, Oslo, 1984).

White, Leigh, *The Long Balkan Night* (Charles Scribner's Sons, New York, 1944).

Woodham Smith, Cecil, *The Great Hunger* (Hamish Hamilton, London, 1975 [first published 1962]).

Worrall, David, *Radical Culture* (Harvester Wheatsheaf, London, 1992).

Also by Annabelle Despard

POETRY

Fisken tenker sitt, Aschehoug 1995

Tyngdekraft, Aschehoug 1995

Bølgende lang som Amerika, Aschehoug 1995

Danseskolen, Cappelen 2005

Dressed in Water, Dionysia 2011

Ved helt riktig måne, Cappelen-Damm, to be published Spring 2015

(In 2014 her poem 'Should You Die First' was selected by London's Southbank Centre as one of the Fifty Best Love Poems of the past 50 years.)

PROSE

Pikeskolen, Portal 2011

OTHER

Impressions with Elisabeth Ibsen and Alf Baartvedt, Aschehoug 1996, 2003, 2008

A Woman's Place: Women, Domesticity and Private Life, (Ed.) Agder College 1998

In Verbo Veritas? (Ed.) Høyskoleforlaget 2002

Texts in Time: British Cutltural Narratives From Defoe to Blair with Jan Erik Mustad and Ulla Rahbek, Fagbokforlaget 2005